Loving Mr. Wright

sex, love & timing

a novella by jillian conley

3

mythreesisters
publishing

ISBN-13: 978-0692251744
ISBN-10: 069225174X

Published by My Three Sisters Publishing

www.my3sisters.com

A fter my three day writing binge in New York City, I decided it was time to head back to Chicago. I couldn't lock myself in a hotel room and ignore reality any longer. I felt sad and disappointed Ben hadn't shown up to meet me on the top of the Empire State Building for my romance movie love plan, but I couldn't escape from reality any longer. The fairy tale I built in my head was just a story and I guess Ben hadn't 'Ben Wright' after all.

The whole flight back to Chicago from New York I was in a daze. I didn't feel like writing anything after writing for three days non-stop, nor was I in the mood for a movie. I closed my eyes and tried to rest. As I was resting and thinking about how the saying 'better late than never' didn't work out for me, I was interrupted by a big splash of water in my face. When I opened my eyes, the rambunctious child in the seat in front of me had taken his water bottle and squirted water at me. I started laughing at what the mischievous little devil of a child had just done and the elderly man in the seat next to me started laughing too.

The child's mother stood up and

apologized for her son's actions when a man in the seat behind me started screaming at the mother because a little water had splashed on him. He was going off, telling the mother that she couldn't control her child and that she was a terrible mother. His screaming interrupted my much needed laugh and I felt bad for the mother so I turned around and said, "Calm down, dude. It's just water," while using my scarf to dry my face.

The guy pointed at the mother and said, "Get your child under control" before he sat down.

I shook my head back and forth a little and the mother apologized for her son's actions over and over. I, along with the man next to me, told her not to worry. She still flagged down the flight attendant to bring us paper towels. Once dried off, I ordered a vodka 7Up to help entertain myself the rest of the flight.

When my plane landed in Chicago, I turned my phone on. I couldn't ignore Nikki and Bree anymore. I read through their texts and they were convinced that Ben and I had run off and gotten married; little did they know that Ben had never shown up at the Empire State Building. While I was getting off the plane, Ben sent me another text asking how I was. I so badly wanted to respond saying that he could've called me to let me know he was never going to show up to save me from making a trip to New York for no reason. I ignored his text and put my phone in my purse while I walked through the airport to a cab.

When I got into a cab, I told the cabbie my address and then pulled my phone back out of my purse. I called Nikki first and she screamed into the phone, "So did you and Ben get hitched? How was it? Tell me every last detail!"

I said, "Hold on. I am going to add Bree to the call."

I dialed Bree and she answered, "Audrey, finally!"

I said, "Hey, Nikki is on too."

Nikki said, "So, tell us all the details."

I said, "Ben never showed up."

Bree said, "Very funny, Audrey."

I said, "Really, he never showed. I waited two and a half hours."

Nikki said, "You are joking, right?"

I said, "I wish I was."

Nikki said, "Did you call him? What was his reason for not showing up?"

I said, "I didn't call him. He called and text me asking me if I was okay, but I never answered."

Nikki asked, "Why the hell didn't you answer? Are you going to call him?"

I said, "I don't feel like talking to him yet so I'll call him back in a few days. I feel angry he didn't show up and I know I have no right to be angry at him. I took too long."

Bree said, "You didn't take too long. You

probably should've kept your pants on and not had sex with those random guys and girl, but if he really wanted to be with you, he should have no problem waiting until you are ready."

Nikki said, "What if something happened to him like in the movie *An Affair to Remember*?"

I said, "He wouldn't have been calling and texting me asking if I was okay if something happened to him."

Nikki said, "Oh yeah, true. Can I call him and ask him what his fucking deal is?"

I said, "No, I'll talk to him when I'm ready."

Nikki said, "I want to know now. What's his number?"

I said, "I'm not giving you his number."

Nikki said, "Fine, I'll just send him a Facebook message."

I said, "Nikki, don't. I want to talk to him calmly like an adult."

Nikki said, "Fine, but hurry up. I want to know what the hell made him go from wanting to marry your ass to totally blowing you off."

Bree said, "I'm really curious about this one, too. He seemed so into you when I met him at your book launch party and from everything you've told us."

I said, "I know and New Year's was perfect so I am totally confused."

Nikki asked, "What the fuck have you been doing the past three days?"

I said, "Writing. I locked myself in the hotel room and wrote."

Nikki asked, "A new story or were you working on the story about the girl who slept her way up to fame?"

I said, "A new story. I actually wrote out the past few months to help me get over Ben."

Nikki asked, "Is that your new thing? Writing memoirs to get over men?"

I said, "No, it's not my new thing."

Bree said, "I think it's great. Writing is good therapy and if it helps Audrey, then she should write out her feelings."

Nikki asked, "Can I read it?"

I said, "No, it's just gibberish."

Nikki said, "Your last piece of gibberish is a best-seller. Let me read it."

I said, "Maybe."

Nikki said, "You should publish it. Write a whole series of memoirs of guys who break your heart."

I said, "Nikki, if I keep writing books about the men who break my heart, I will never get married. All guys will be afraid to date me because I might write about them."

Nikki said, "Good point. I still want to read what you wrote."

Bree interrupted asking, "Where are you now, Audrey?"

I said, "In a cab on my way home."

Bree said, "Come over to my place."

I said, "I kind of just want to go home.

I'm tired and I just want to regroup."

Bree said, "Come on. You guys never come over to my place. Scotty is out of town. I'll cook us dinner, we can drink some wine, and we can go down to the indoor pool and hot tub in my building."

I said, "Fine, but give me a couple hours to go home and relax."

Nikki said, "Does this mean I have to come too?"

Bree said, "Yes, Nikki."

Nikki said, "Fine, but I ain't shaving my legs for the pool."

I said, "I'm not shaving mine either."

Nikki said, "Audrey, your legs should be shaved. Didn't you shave them for Ben?"

I said, "Yes, but that was four days ago so I have some scruff."

Nikki said, "Fuck, yeah, in four days all my leg hair would have grown back. I'm going on a week so I'm really hairy."

Bree said, "Oh, my God, you guys, I don't care how hairy your legs are."

Nikki responded, "Coming from the blonde who probably shaves once a fucking month."

I condescendingly asked, "Right? Bree, you are lucky you aren't hairy like us."

Bree said, "I deal with hair, but I just don't talk about it all the time."

I asked, "Do you have a notorious nipple hair?"

Bree said, "No, I don't have nipple hairs."

Nikki said, "You lucky bitch."

Bree said, "Alright, enough hair talk. I'll see you guys in T minus two hours. Don't be late!"

I got home and went right into the bathroom. I sat down on the toilet and thought about how good it feels to take a shit at home after traveling. I pulled my phone off the bathroom counter and caught up on what was happening on Twitter. I responded to a few fans and tweeted out a link to my latest blog post. After I tweeted out the link to my latest blog post, I searched the hashtag #twitterontheshitter to see if anyone else was tweeting while they pooped. I found quite a few, which entertained me for a hot second.

After I was finished pooping, I went and lay on my bed and closed my eyes to rest for a little bit. I ended up dozing off and woke up to my phone ringing non-stop. I knew it was Nikki from the ringtone and when I looked at the clock I thought: *Fuck. I fell asleep!* I jumped out of bed while answering the phone. Nikki said, "Dude, I'm in a cab downstairs."

I said, "I'll be right down. Sorry, I dozed off."

Nikki said, "I figured. Hurry up. The meter is on."

I took a bathing suit out of my drawer and then grabbed my purse as I walked toward the door. I locked my front door and ran down the stairs. When I got in the cab I said, "Sorry, I didn't think I'd fall asleep."

Nikki said, "Its fine. Why the hell are we swimming when it's five degrees outside?"

I said, "It's an indoor pool and we never go to her place. She's excited to be having us over so let's just go and get drunk."

Nikki said, "Christ, the last thing a girl wants to do in the middle of the winter is put on a God damn bathing suit."

I said, "It's just us girls so no need to impress anyone."

Nikki said, "I ain't going to be impressing anyone with these hairy legs and holiday stomach pouch."

I said, "Christmas was like a month ago."

Nikki said, "Shut up, skinny ass. Holiday pouches last until St. Patrick's Day. I don't have to get my ass into the gym until then."

Nikki and I arrived at Bree's and she was super bubbly when she welcomed us into her apartment. It was a bit too much cheer for me, but she was excited and I wanted to be a good friend so I smiled. She had appetizers out and wine already poured so I was happy we decided to come. I took my glass of wine and sat down on the couch next to the hummus and pita bread. I started stuffing my face with the snacks Bree had out for us. She told me not to eat too much because after we went in the hot tub, we'd be having her homemade lasagna. Coming to Bree's was turning out to be a great decision.

We ate appetizers, sat in the hot tub, ate lasagna, and drank way too much wine. I wanted to be home alone pouting in my bed, but time laughing with my two best friends was the best therapy for me. We talked about Ben a little bit, but we stayed off the topic most of the night. I promised them I'd call Ben the next day and find out why he decided not to show up.

A little after midnight Nikki and I headed home. I was exhausted and couldn't wait to crawl into bed. When the cab pulled up to my building Nikki asked, "Are you going to shower before bed?"

I said, "Probably not. I'm pooped and we were just in chlorinated water. I think I am just going to go hit the sheets."

Nikki said, "You should shower and shave your legs."

I said, "Why the fuck would I shave my legs before I go to bed alone?"

"Just do it. Good luck."

I asked, "Why are you wishing me luck?"

Nikki hugged me as she said, "Never mind. Goodnight."

I got out of the cab and walked up to my apartment wondering what was up with Nikki. I was exhausted and drunk so I didn't dwell on it long. I brushed my teeth, threw on some pajamas and crawled into bed. I was asleep in a matter of seconds. I woke up early the next morning and turned on my laptop. I curled back into bed and caught up on emails from my PR agent, Steven, who was getting frustrated that I hadn't returned his calls. As I was emailing him back confirming travel dates, Nikki called. I answered, "Good morning."

Nikki said, "Go open your front door."

I asked, "Are you here?"

Nikki said, "Just go open your front door. Call me back later."

I said, "Okay, but why do you want me to open my door?"

"Just go open it, asshole, and call me later. Bye."

After Nikki hung up on me, I put my phone down on my nightstand and walked to the front door. I opened the door and there was an open box of donuts on the ground with frosting spelling out, "I luv u 2." In the middle of the box was a miniature Empire State Building. I looked down the hall and didn't see anyone. I thought to myself what a cruel, yet sweet thing for Nikki to do. As I bent over to pick up the box of delicious loving donuts, Ben appeared at the top of the stairs. I left the donuts on the ground, jumping over the box to run to him. When I got close, I jumped up and wrapped my legs around him before I kissed him. He kissed me back, carrying me while he walked us into my apartment. He kicked the box of donuts into my apartment and then kicked the door closed behind us.

Once inside, we continued kissing. I felt

so happy to be in his arms and lip locked with him. I didn't even need an explanation for him not showing up at the Empire State Building, I was just happy he was here at that moment. I knew eventually I'd find out why he wasn't there to meet me that night. Ben walked us into my bedroom and dropped his bag on the ground before laying me down on the bed and crawling on top of me. I smiled at him and he smiled back before kissing me again. As we kissed, Ben caressed my breasts over my shirt before moving his hand down to rub my pussy outside of my sweatpants. I thought *crap, my muff has scruff and my legs were scruffy, too. Damn it! This was a movie-like moment and here I was all hairy and not showered. How come in the movies women were always prepared by being dressed nice and clean shaven for moments like these?* I said to Ben, "My muff is hairy."

Ben laughed a little and said, "I don't care."

I asked, "Can I go shave it real quick?"

Ben said, "Don't ruin the moment. A little scruff doesn't bother me" as he took his coat off. He leaned back down and got back to kissing me.

While we continued passionately kissing, our clothing slowly came off. I felt a sense of excitement and happy horniness running through my body. I was so glad to have Ben on top of me, holding me, and kissing me. Once our clothes were all off, Ben penetrated my scruffy pussy. I smiled at him as I put both my hands on his face and said, "I love you."

Ben said, "I love you too, Audrey."

Ben slowly moved his cock in and out of my pussy and I could feel it getting harder with each thrust inside of me while my pussy got wet. My hands were still on Ben's face when I pulled him down to kiss me more. I couldn't get enough of his kisses and I kept smiling while we were kissing. I wrapped my legs around his back and enjoyed the pleasure of him inside of me. When he started moving faster, I could feel my pussy tightening. I used my legs to pull my hips off the bed and that's when his cock started hitting my G spot head on. I whispered in his ear, "Faster."

Ben moved his cock in and out of my pussy faster and faster and moments later my pussy tightened up and then released an orgasm, pulsating in pleasure. As I was coming, I felt Ben cum inside of me while releasing an orgasmic moan. After he finished orgasming, he kissed me on the forehead before lying down on the bed next to me. I turned to him and asked, "Ben, why didn't you show up at the Empire State Building the other night?"

Ben said, "Cause your note said January twenty-ninth at 5pm."

I said, "No, it said January twentieth."

Ben said, "I have the note in my bag. It really says the twenty-ninth."

I said, "Oh my goodness, it must've been

a typo and they pressed nine instead of zero! So you were planning to be there?"

Ben said, "Of course I was planning to be there. I started getting worried because you were ignoring all my calls and text messages so yesterday evening I sent Nikki a message on Facebook to make sure you were okay. She messaged me back asking why I didn't show up at the Empire State Building and that's when we figured out the date was wrong on the note. After I talked to her, I booked the next flight to Chicago."

I said, "Oh, so that's why she told me I should shower and shave my legs last night."

Ben said, "I wish you would've listened to her. I think I have rug burn on my dick."

I lightly hit Ben as I said, "Shut up! I warned you."

Ben said, "I'm only kidding, your box is perfect."

I asked, "My box?"

"Yes, your box."

"Did you just call my pussy a box?"

"Yes."

"That's hilarious."

Ben said, "So now what, Audrey?"

I said, "Now we eat donuts, Mr. Wright."

Ben asked, "Why are you so afraid to talk about us?"

I said, "I'm not. What do you need to know? I love you, you love me, and we are in love."

Ben said, "Are you forgetting we live in different states?"

I said, "Ben, let's eat some donuts and enjoy this lovely moment."

B en and I spent the entire day inside laughing, eating and having sex. I felt a happiness that I had never felt before. The next morning, I woke up to Ben watching me sleep. After I opened my eyes, I rubbed them as I asked, "What are you looking at?"

Ben said, "Your beautiful face."

I lightly waved my hand at him and said, "You are goofy."

Ben said, "Marry me."

I asked for him to repeat what he just said to ensure I heard him right by asking, "What?"

"Marry me, Audrey Buchanan!"

I let out a little laugh as I repeated, "You are goofy."

Ben said, "Marry me, you beautiful girl! Marry me!"

I was totally taken aback. I had just gotten used to the idea of dating this man and now he wanted me to marry him. I said, "You are crazy, Mr. Wright."

"Marry me and make me the happiest man in the world. Come on, let's go to Tiffany's and get you a ring."

I said, "You are silly."

Ben said, "I am serious. I'll go to Las Vegas with you tomorrow for your book signings and we can get married there."

"I'm not getting married in Las Vegas!"

"Why not? It could be fun."

"I've always wanted to get married on a beach."

"Alright, we'll go to the Caribbean and get married after your book signings in Las Vegas."

I said, "You are goofy, but if you fuck me right now, I'll consider it."

Ben threw the covers off him and said, "My dick is already hard. Let's do this," before he crawled on top of me and penetrated my pussy. As Ben was fucking me, it was hard to concentrate. Did he really just ask me to marry him? This was crazy. Was I ready to marry him? Was I even ready to get married in general? As my mind was frantically contemplating marriage, Ben said, "Just say yes and stop thinking about it."

I'd be a fool not to marry Ben so I smiled and said, "Yes, yes, I will marry you, Mr. Wright!"

Ben stopped penetrating my pussy, leaned his head down and kissed me before he said, "Audrey, we are going to have a blast!"

I said, "I know. Now, keep fucking me, my hot fiancé!"

Ben said, "Anything you say, my beautiful fiancé!"

After a few minutes of fucking missionary

style, I moved on my side to have Ben spoon me and fuck me from behind. He followed my lead and I was grateful because I loved the way his cock hit my G spot during a good slow motion spoon fuck. Ben held me tight as he penetrated my pussy from behind. As he was penetrating me, I could feel happiness running through my body. I wasn't sure what I was getting myself into by saying yes to marrying him, but I knew that whatever journey I was about to embark on, I had made the right choice of man to embark on it with.

After we both orgasmed, we lay relaxing for a few moments before getting up to shower. Ben wanted to go to lunch and get out for a little bit of fresh air and sunshine. I agreed that it would be good since I had locked myself in a hotel room in New York for a few days. Once showered, we headed out to lunch on Michigan Avenue. After we finished lunch, Ben insisted we take a little walk. Of course, Ben strategically ended our little walk at Tiffany's. Since I had said yes, I couldn't disagree that a ring was needed to seal the deal.

We walked into Tiffany's and immediately a woman approached us before asking, "Mr. and soon to be Mrs. Wright?"

Ben replied, "That's us."

The woman said, "Follow me."

We followed the woman to the back of the store where she sat us down on a couch and brought us champagne. I leaned over to Ben and asked, "How does she know us?"

Ben said, "I called them while you were in the shower. Only the best for you, baby." Ben caught himself remembering the outburst I had because my ex-boyfriend Chase always called me 'baby' and said, "Wait, no 'baby.' I'm sorry. Only the best for you, darling."

I said, "This is crazy."

Ben said, "Crazy fun! Let's get you the best ring in here."

I gave Ben a kiss and said, "I don't know how I scored you, but I am so glad I wasn't too late."

Ben said, "I'm glad you figured it out because I would've asked you to marry me the day we were in Tiffany's in New York if I didn't think it would scare you away."

"Yes, that would've freaked me out. Are you sure about this Ben?"

"Audrey, do you think I'd be about to pay a hundred grand on a ring if I wasn't sure?"

I said, "A ring doesn't cost a hundred grand."

Ben said, "We need to get you an exceptional ring. I'm sure a hundred grand is the starting rate."

I said, "Ben, I don't need a big ring."

Ben said, "You don't need it, but a beautiful girl like you deserves a ring as beautiful as I see you."

I said, "This is insane. Save that money for a house or some shit."

Ben said, "Darling, a hundred grand is chump change for me. Let's pick you out a beauty."

The woman sat down with us and asked about what kind of ring I wanted. I told her round cut with a thin simple band. I didn't want something crazy big, but with each ring that the woman brought us, the diamonds seemed to be getting bigger. Ben wanted a big ring for me, but I told him over and over that I had a tendency to lose things. He was insistent that this was something that I wouldn't lose.

I ended up picking out a four carat diamond with a thin band. It was brilliantly shiny. After we walked out of Tiffany's, I looked at the ring on my finger and then asked Ben, "Now what?"

Ben said, "It's time to tell the parents."

I thought to myself: *Holy shit, I had never met Ben's family. I said yes to marry a man and have never met his family. What was I doing? My parents had met Ben at my book launch and loved him, but the meeting was brief.* I said to Ben, "My mom is going to be ecstatic."

Ben said, "My mom is going to be, too."

I asked, "What if your mom doesn't like me?"

Ben said, "She's going to love you!"

I said, "God, I hope so."

Ben said, "Call your parents and tell them to come downtown for dinner tonight. I'll go to Las Vegas with you tomorrow for your book signings and then we can fly to California to tell my family."

I said, "This is absolutely nutty."

Ben responded, "It's going to be great. Call your parents."

I took out my phone and called my mom to ask if she and my father could come downtown for dinner. She said she was just about to put a pot roast in the oven so I told her that Ben and I were going to come out to their house for dinner. She got excited and told me to pick up a dessert, preferably a pie, on our way. I agreed. After I hung up the phone, I realized that I no longer had a car after my ex-boyfriend Chase's girlfriend vandalized it. I said, "Ben, I don't have a car to get us to my parents' house."

Ben said, "That's okay. We will take a limo."

I said, "Ben, we are not taking a limo to my parent's house. It's over an hour away."

"Why not? We can fuck in the back."

I smiled and said, "Did you really just say fuck?"

Ben said, "Now that we are engaged I have to get used to swearing because I know you like it. Let's get a limo and fuck in it."

I jokingly said, "Your swearing does turn me on."

Ben and I went back to my apartment and he called to order a limo while I changed. The limo arrived on time and once we got in Ben closed the window to the front and said, "Let's get naked!"

I laughed before Ben put his right hand on

my face and pulled me in for a kiss. I kissed him back while I started to unbutton his coat. We kissed as we removed our layers of clothing and once we were both naked, Ben put one hand on the back of my head before guiding me to lie on my back. Once on my back, Ben penetrated my pussy. I moaned in pleasure. He slowly moved in and out of my pussy as I got more wet with each thrust. Once I could see my cum on his cock as he moved in and out of me, I pushed him to sit on the seat and then I sat down on his cock. I moved up and down, but I wanted to move higher so I opened the sunroof to allow me more moving room as I rode Ben's cock. The snow fell on us, but I didn't feel cold because I was so turned on.

I continued moving up and down on Ben's cock faster and faster as he held onto my breasts from behind. Ben whispered in a sexy tone, "Ride my cock."

I listened and bounced up and down faster, trying to position myself so his cock would directly hit my G spot. Once it did, my pussy got tighter with each bounce. My pussy became tight and I moaned out, "I'm going to cum" and as my pussy started pulsating I felt Ben's cock cum at the same time, creating an even more euphoric orgasm for me.

After our orgasms, I moved to sit on the seat next to Ben to enjoy coming down from my orgasm. As we sat together catching our breaths, the snow continued to fall on us from the open sunroof. Ben said, "I'd close the sunroof, but the cold feels good on my hot body."

I said, "It feels good on mine, too. I was doing all the work!"

Ben said, "Hey now, I'm the one usually putting in the work."

I said, "That's because you love doing it missionary style."

Ben said, "I just love looking at your beautiful face when we have sex. Excuse me, when we fuck."

I said, "I like that your language is getting dirtier."

Ben said, "Anything to make you happy, bride."

"Bride, very funny, Mr. Wright."

"You are my bride. So where do you want to get married?"

I said, "Let's get the approval of our families before we start discussing logistics."

Ben said, "Your family is going to be ecstatic and so is mine so let's start planning."

I said, "You are totally the girl in this relationship."

Ben jokingly said, "Hey, now" before he gently kissed me on the forehead.

I said, "Do you want to plan the wedding? I'd totally be cool with that because I have no desire to plan a wedding. Or, I'm sure my mom would love to do it for us."

"Audrey, you are not like most girls."

I jokingly asked, "Are you just figuring this out now?"

"No, it's actually why I fell in love with you."

"So it's a good thing!"

"It's the best thing, but I want you to have the wedding of your dreams. I want the day to be perfect for us."

"I'll tell you my perfect idea of a wedding, but only because I love you."

"Okay, what is it?"

I said, "No planning. No rush. No hoopla. No expensive flowers. No crazy registry. No big bridal party. And finally, not in Chicago."

"What about the dress?"

"The dress, well that is something I already have designed in my head, but I can't tell you about it because you are the groom."

"You are such a tease!"

I said, "I am no tease. I'll put out for you right now if you want."

Ben said, "You have the libido of a college boy."

I said, "Get used to it because I am the only girl you will be sleeping with for the rest of your life."

"And that makes me the luckiest guy in the world."

As Ben and I were redressing, I realized I had been sitting on his shirt leaving a big cum stain on the front of it. We started laughing not knowing how we were going to cover it up. We tried using water to wipe it off, but it created a big wet spot. He asked, "What am I going to tell your parents? You came on my chest?"

I said, "Well, it is the truth," as I laughed. I continued on by saying, "Hold on, I have an idea."

I grabbed a glass of champagne and threw in on Ben. He said, "Why the heck did you do that?"

I said, "We can tell my parents I spilled champagne on you. They know how clumsy I am so they will believe it."

"My chest is going to freeze."

"It's like a ten second walk into my parents' house from the driveway."

The limo pulled into my parents' driveway and Ben asked, "Wait, how do we want to tell them that we are engaged?"

I said, "I don't know. Shouldn't we just walk in and show them the ring?"

Ben said, "If that's how you want to do it."

I asked, "What, do you want me to hide it in the pot roast or something?"

Ben said, "Oh no, we forgot the pie!"

"Crap, we did forget the pie! Oh well, I'm sure my mom has something. Otherwise, we can run out after dinner."

"Alright, so we are going to walk in together and after we take our coats off, you are going to show them the ring, right?"

"Correcto mundo, Ben. You ready?"

"Is it weird I'm a little nervous?"

"Ben, you don't have to be nervous around my parents."

"I know they are really laid back. I remember talking to your father at your book launch. I just feel bad I didn't ask him for his permission to marry you before I asked you."

I said, "Then ask him tonight."

Ben took my hand to help me out of the limo and we kept holding hands walking through the snow up to my parents' door. I opened their front door up and immediately heard my mother yell from the kitchen, "Audrey, is that you?"

I said, "Yes, Mom, it's me."

She screamed back and asked, "Did you get a pie?"

I said, "No, I forgot so I'll run out after dinner."

As my mom walked toward the foyer she said, "I thought you might forget, but luckily I found a frozen cherry pie in the freezer. I'll heat that up."

I said, "Sorry, I forgot. We had a very busy day."

My mom said, "It's okay. I'm just so happy to have you here for dinner," as she gave me a kiss. She then moved in toward Ben and said, "Give me a hug, you."

My mother was being abnormally nice. Last guy I brought home was Chase and she barely noticed our presence. She must've known something was up. I asked, "Where's Dad?"

All of a sudden my father popped his head out from around the corner and said, "I'm right here, bug," before he put his hand out and said, "Great to see you again, Ben."

I said, "Good, I'm glad you are both here because I, I mean we, have something to tell you. I'm pregnant."

Both my parents jaws dropped and they were quiet for a few moments before my mom began jumping up and down in excitement. She said, "I'm going to be a grandmother! A baby is a blessing no matter how it comes. I know times are changing and having a bastard child is okay."

I said, "Mom, you can't say bastard anymore."

My mom said, "Isn't that what a child born out of wedlock is?" She looked at my father and continued, "Right, dear? That's what a bastard is."

My dad said, "Yes, but Audrey is right. We shouldn't call her child a bastard."

I said, "I'm just kidding. We aren't having a baby." I walked past them and as I walked into the living room I asked, "When will dinner be ready?"

My mom said, "Audrey, that isn't funny" before she said to Ben, "Let me take your coat." She took off Ben's coat and said, "Oh dear, you are all wet. What happened?"

Ben said, "Audrey spilled a little

champagne on me in the limo on the way here."

My mom said, "You took a limousine out here?"

I cut in and said, "Yes, because we were celebrating."

My mom asked, "Celebrating what?"

I held up my left hand and said, "We are engaged, Mom!"

My mom dropped Ben's coat on the ground and ran over to me. She screamed out, "Oh my goodness, look at the size of that ring!" She then looked at my father and said, "And we thought this day was never going to happen for Audrey! I'm so excited!"

I said, "Wait, Mom, you thought I would never get married?"

My mom said, "Well, to be honest I would rather you spend your life as a spinster over marrying some of the men you've dated. Especially that Chase Walker guy. The only good thing he ever did for you was to get you to write that story."

I said, "Thanks, Mom."

My mom walked over to Ben and said, "I knew you were a catch when we met you at Audrey's book launch. Thank you for your patience with my daughter. I prayed every day, hoping she'd see what was right in front of her."

I cut in and asked, "You prayed?"

My mom said, "Yes, I prayed. Just because we aren't church goers doesn't mean I don't pray. All I've ever wanted was a nice boy for you and look at this strapping young man. I hear you are rich too, Ben."

I said, "Mom, don't talk to him about his money."

Ben said, "It's okay, Audrey. Mrs. Buchanan, I have plenty of money to take care of your daughter if that is your concern."

My mom said, "No, no, call me 'Mom!'"

Ben said, "Okay, Mom."

My dad said, "This calls for a drink. I have a forty year old bottle of scotch I've been keeping for a celebration like this."

My mom said, "Good, honey, you go get the scotch. Ben, come with me and I'll get you a dry shirt. I know of one that's perfect for you."

My dad went one way and Ben and my mom went the other way. I decided to take a seat on the couch and wait for everyone to come back. A few minutes later, Ben came out wearing my father's famous "I heart Audrey" shirt. It was a shirt with a picture on the front of me when I was four years old. I said, "Oh, my God, Mom, you didn't make Ben wear Dad's 'I heart Audrey' t-shirt!"

Ben smiled at me and laughed as my mom said, "It's perfect. He does love you. I want a picture of you two while he's wearing it. I think it will make a great engagement photo!"

I said, "Mom, we are not taking an engagement photo with Ben wearing this."

Ben said, "I like the shirt. It's comfortable. I think we should take a photo in it."

I said, "Oh, geeze. Fine!"

Ben and I smiled for the camera as my mom took a picture of us. She made me hold my left hand up to show off my engagement ring and it was uber cheesy. It was our first photo ever as a couple, which was strange to think. We became a couple pretty much when we got engaged. I started thinking I was crazy and my face must've showed it because Ben asked if I was okay. I smiled at him, gave him a kiss, and said, "Of course."

After our photo my mom sat down with us to check out my ring under a light. She asked if we had picked a date. I reminded her we had just gotten engaged that morning so we hadn't even thought of a date. Ben explained that he wanted to elope right away, but I wanted to be engaged for awhile. My mom agreed that a longer engagement would give her more time to plan. I told her a big wedding was not necessary and she said of course it was because I was their only child. That's when I realized all the perks of being an only child were about to bite me in the ass.

My father toasted to us with glasses of his forty year old bottle of scotch, which tasted totally wicked and then we ate dinner and dessert. My mom was so excited about the engagement that she never wanted us to leave, but I told her we had a long drive back to the city and that we had to fly to Las Vegas in the morning. She made me promise a good ten times that we would not elope in Las Vegas. Her insistence made me want to elope.

When Ben and I got back to my apartment, he crawled into bed with his laptop to get a seat on my flight while I called Nikki and Bree to tell them the engagement news. They were excited, but Bree, a girl who never reveals any ounce of jealousy kept saying over and over that she couldn't believe I was going to get married before her. I couldn't blame her for her confusion. She had been in a long-term relationship for years with Scotty Stylez and hoped each day he'd finally propose.

After a good hour on the phone with Nikki and Bree, I walked into my bedroom. Ben was on my bed asleep with his glasses on and laptop on his stomach. He looked adorable, lying there sleeping. I walked up to him and took his laptop off his lap and then slowly took his glasses off before crawling into bed next to him. When I crawled into bed he woke up for a moment and pulled me toward him to hold me tight. I smiled, wondering how I got so lucky to find a man like Ben to love me.

Ben agreed with my decision not to tell my PR agent, Steven, about the engagement. I felt his family should know before we told anyone else. I also knew that the moment Steven found out he would start thinking of ways to use our engagement to publicize my book. Ben expressed concern because I was holding back from telling people we were engaged. Ben was onto me. I was excited, I truly was, but I needed a few more days to let it all sink in because everything was happening so fast. I told Ben he didn't have to worry and we could tell the world once his family knew.

We checked into the Cosmo Hotel in Las Vegas and when we got into our room I asked Ben, "Do you want to have a quickie before the bellman gets here with our luggage?"

Ben said, "Last person to get naked is on top!"

I laughed at Ben and quickly undressed. I purposely lost though. I wanted to be on top. I loved Ben being on top, and it seemed like he was always on top so I wanted to mix it up a bit. Once I was fully naked, Ben pulled me close to him and kissed me for a few moments before crashing down on the bed on his back. His cock was hard and sticking straight up when he pointed to it and said, "Jump on, darling."

I said, "Hold on. I need to get more wet," before I licked my fingers and then put them down on my pussy. I slowly moved my fingers over my pussy and Ben sat up to watch me. As I rubbed my labia up and down with my right hand, I caressed my left boob with my left hand.

Ben said, "This is hot. Keep going."

I kept moving my fingers around and it felt good. As I was rubbing my clit, there was a knock on the door. I stopped and said, "Shit, the bellman is already here."

Ben yelled to the door, "One moment" before getting up, grabbing my hips, and penetrating me from behind. He pushed his cock in and out of my pussy literally only six times before he came, ran over to the closet, grabbed a robe and opened the door for the bellman. After Ben pulled our luggage into the room, I gave him a 'What the fuck?' look. He asked, "What?"

I said, "What the hell was that? It was like the world's fastest fuck."

Ben said, "You said you wanted a quickie."

I said, "I also said I wanted to be on top. You ran up behind me and fucked me like a caveman."

Ben said, "You masturbating was such a turn on and I panicked when I heard knocking on the door." Ben walked over to me and continued, "Lie down on the bed, darling. We won't leave this room until I get you off with my tongue."

I said, "Okay, this is more like it."

I lay down on the bed and Ben crawled in between my legs with a smile. When he put his tongue on my labia, I moaned in pleasure before closing my eyes and taking in the sensation of pleasure being sent through my body. As he was moving his tongue around my labia, he inserted a finger in my pussy. He said, "You are so wet. I can feel my cum inside of you."

I thought to myself that it was strange for him to say he could feel his cum inside of me, but I decided to forget his words and concentrate on him pleasuring me. He licked the top of my clit while slowly moving his finger in and out of my pussy with pressure on the top. It felt amazing, but I encouraged him to pick up speed. As he moved faster, the pleasure increased more and more, causing my pussy to gradually feel tighter. Once it was too tight for me to hold on any longer, I released an orgasm. When my pussy was finished twitching, Ben said, "Watching you cum is the most beautiful thing in the world."

I whispered, "Feeling myself cum is the most amazing feeling in the world. Let's make a pact to have sex everyday for the rest of our lives, fiancé."

Ben laughed when he said, "Can we put that

in our vows?"

I said, "I'm sure your mother would love to hear us say that in our vows."

The next two days, I was gone all day long at book signings and events. Ben spent the days and much of the nights in the room working on his laptop. He did a lot of business in London so he worked odd hours. He wanted to get as much done as possible so we could relax and enjoy time with his mother and sister in California.

When we landed at John Wayne Airport in California, I felt uneasiness in my stomach. I was suddenly extremely nervous to meet Ben's mother and sister. The vodka 7Up I drank on the short flight from Las Vegas wasn't enough to calm my nerves. As we stood waiting for our rental car at the airport I said to Ben, "My stomach feels weird. I'm really nervous."

Ben said, "Don't be. My family is great and they are going to love you."

I took some deep breaths trying to calm my mind and stomach, but it wasn't helping. We got into our rental car and started driving toward his sister's house in Laguna Beach. When we got on Pacific Coast Highway, I looked out the window to enjoy the beautiful view. Ben said, "Isn't it beautiful here? I hope to move back here one day. Would you want to live in California?"

I said, "It is beautiful. I would definitely consider moving here."

Ben said, "Good, we'll retire here" then he

continued by singing, "Will you still need me, will you still feed me when I'm sixty-four?"

I laughed at him singing the Beatles song before I said, "Of course. You are going to be stuck with me forever, mister!"

Ben said, "Forever. I like that," before he leaned over and kissed me.

We were quiet for a few minutes when my stomach really started rumbling and felt queasy. I couldn't ignore it any longer. A little sweat built up on my upper lip and I felt like I was about to have diarrhea. I said, "Ben, we have to pull over at a gas station right now."

Ben asked, "Why? Do you have to pee? We are almost to my sister's. It's only ten minutes away."

I said, "No, we need to stop NOW."

Ben asked, "Can't you hold it?"

I said, "No, Ben I have to shit, now! Like I think I might have diarrhea!"

Ben said, "Oh, okay. I'll hurry."

Ben sped down the road, laughing the entire time before pulling over at the first gas station he saw. I ran out of the car, clenching my butt cheeks tight until I got into the disgusting gas station bathroom. Once inside a stall, I hovered over the toilet and released the hot diarrhea out of my ass. I could feel the rest of my body cooling down almost immediately following the release.

I walked out of the bathroom to the car. Ben had his head out the window and was smiling at me. I smiled back and started laughing, causing him to laugh. When I got into the car Ben asked, "Do you feel better now?"

I said, "Yes, I feel a thousand times better. I must be really nervous."

Ben said, "Stop being nervous. My family is going to fall in love with you. I've heard singing helps relax people."

I said, "Ben, I should warn you now that I am tone deaf. Like, really bad. I can't sing a note."

As Ben was flipping through the radio stations he said, "Oh, come on, you can't be that bad."

I said, "Trust me, I'm that bad."

Ben yelled out, "Oh yeah, this is the perfect song to loosen you up and it talks about butts!"

Ben turned up the radio and *Baby Got Back* by Sir-Mix-A lot was playing. He started singing along and I laughed. He kept telling me to sing too and I resisted for as long as I could, but when you hear *Baby Got Back* it's only natural to start moving your body and singing along. After the song ended, Ben turned down the radio and we laughed. Smiling, I said, "Okay, that did make me feel better."

Ben said, "I told you it would." He laughed a little before he continued, "You weren't kidding about your voice though."

I smacked his shoulder a little as I said, "Shut up!"

We arrived at Ben's sister house and when

we pulled up, I was shocked to find she lived in a huge mansion. I mean enormous. I mean ridiculously large. I knew Ben was rich, but his sister was, too. I asked, "Is your whole family rich?"

Ben laughed before he said, "My sister married well, very well."

We walked up to the mansion hand-in-hand, but before we walked inside Ben said, "You are beautiful and I love you."

I gave him a little kiss and said, "I love you, too."

Ben opened the door as his niece ran up to him and jumped on him. She screamed, "Uncle Ben! Uncle Ben! Guess what? I got a dog. A real life dog and I named him Jasper. Do you like the name, Jasper? I thought of it myself. Who's this lady with you? She's pretty."

I smiled at the little girl and was grateful that she called me pretty. Ben said, "This is Audrey, Carly."

Carly said, "Hello, Audrey."

I said, "Hello, Carly. I love your shoes."

Carly said, "I wore them because Uncle Ben bought them for me. They are the same shoes that Dorothy wore in the movie *The Wizard of Oz*. Have you seen *The Wizard of Oz*, Audrey? If not, we can watch it."

I said, "I haven't seen that movie in a really long time so I'd love to watch it with you."

Carly took both our hands and led us into the living room where his sister and mother were sitting. They each had a glass of wine in their hands, which made me think to myself: *Thank God!* I really needed a drink. Ben introduced me to his mom, Sherry and his sister, Catherine. His mother, Sherry looked like a simple lady. She had short gray hair and wore a cute white pantsuit. Ben's sister, Catherine was absolutely gorgeous. She was tall, thin, with dark black hair and bright blue eyes. I wouldn't have been surprised if I found out later that she was a Victoria's Secret model. We all sat down in unison and then Carly asked if she could get us drinks. I thought: *Fuck how could I ask this five year old for a glass of wine?* Ben must've known what I was thinking and said, "Let me get those drinks with you, Carly, because I want a big boy drink."

Carly said, "That means you want a beer, Uncle Ben. I know what big boy drinks are."

Ben walked out of the room and the room became silent. I said, "This is a beautiful house, Catherine."

Catherine softly replied, "Thank you."

There were more moments of awkward silence until Sherry said, "Benny has been talking about you non-stop for the past couple of months, Audrey. It's nice to finally meet you in person."

I said, "I've been looking forward to meeting the both of you, too."

Sherry said, "I saw you on *Good Morning America* a little while back and I read your book, *Dating Chase Walker.*" I thought to myself: *Shit, my future mother-in-law read my book about me having sex with my ex-boyfriend. This was not a good start to the weekend.* Sherry continued, "I was surprised how engaged I was while reading it." I gulped a little when I heard her say the word 'engaged.' Sherry continued, "I wasn't going to buy it because it's not my usual style of reading material, but when Benny said he knew you, I thought I'd tune in."

Catherine interjected saying, "It sure is graphic."

I said, "My work is pretty erotic, but it seems to be a style of writing I'm good at."

Catherine asked, "So do you only write about sex?"

I said, "I also have a freelance job with a local newspaper." I laughed a little as I said, "The material I write for them is generally pretty clean."

Before Sherry or Catherine could say anything further, Ben and Carly walked back into the room, singing. Ben handed me a glass of wine and then he asked, "So what are you girls talking about?"

Catherine said, "We were just discussing Audrey's writing."

Ben said, "Audrey is a brilliant writer." He then switched the conversation quickly asking, "When will Bo be home?"

I wondered to myself who the fuck Bo was,

but figured it was Catherine's husband. I really should have learned more about Ben's family before meeting them. Catherine said, "He will be back for dinner."

We sat and talked for another hour or so. I was drilled with questions, but it was much easier to deal with because Ben kept my wine glass full. He was going to make a great husband. When the sun was starting to set, Ben took me out back to watch the sunset. It was beautiful. We cuddled on a chair and Carly crawled between us to watch it, too. Three of us on a chair made it a little cramped and Carly was pushing on my bladder so as soon as the sun was down, I got up to go to the bathroom. It was time to release all the wine I had consumed in the past couple of hours.

On my way back from the bathroom, I ran into Bo Brady in the hallway. Bo Brady, the most famous actor in Hollywood. I was star struck when Bo said, "Oh, you must be the famous Audrey!"

Famous Bo Brady just called me fucking famous. I was in shock. I said, "I am Audrey."

Bo came close to me and I felt my stomach drop being in such close proximity with the biggest name in Hollywood when he said, "I heard about the engagement. Where is the ring?"

I said, "I'm not putting it on until after Ben tells Catherine and Sherry at dinner."

Bo said, "I see. Make sure you get drunk

first. Want to do a shot with me? I feel like I have some catching up to do."

I said, "I'd love a shot."

Bo and I went into his office and drank our shots out of large crystal glasses. The entire time I was in the office I couldn't help but think how Nikki was going to freak out when she found out I was with Bo Brady. I also couldn't believe that Ben didn't tell me his brother-in-law was Bo Brady. Actually, that seemed just like Ben not to tell me something like that. I still couldn't believe that I was going to be related to Bo Brady.

After our large shots of whiskey, we went out to the kitchen where Ben and Carly were sitting down at the table. Ben looked at me smiling before standing up and inviting me over by pulling out a chair for me. I sat down and Ben picked up my wine glass to refill. My love for him just kept growing stronger. Ben brought back my glass full of wine and sat down next to me. Once seated, he leaned over and said, "I have your ring in my pocket. I'll give it to you after I tell everyone the good news."

I winked at Ben and said, "Okay, I'll follow your lead."

The salad came out and then the main entrée and Ben hadn't dropped the bomb about our engagement. I started wondering when he was going to say something and I think his brother-in-law, Bo, started wondering too because he kept looking at Ben. Finally, when

Carly was putting "sprinkles" on our dessert, Ben said he had something exciting to tell everyone and he announced that he and I were going to get married. His mother clapped her hands in excitement, but his sister didn't say much. In fact, her wine glass seemed to become glued to her lip, which was the same tendency I had when I was unsure about something.

Ben took my engagement ring out of his pocket and put it on my finger. I showed it off around the table and everyone seemed impressed with the size, especially Carly. She said it shined like the sun. It was an exciting few minutes. After dinner, Ben and I went into the pool house to get ready for bed. It was a long day of traveling and I was exhausted. I could've fallen asleep in a few minutes, but as we were changing for bed, I took a look at Ben and saw his hot body. I walked over to him while he was changing and kissed him. Our standing kiss soon moved to the bed and after many minutes of warm kisses, he started moving his lips down my neck and onto my breasts. He continued heading south when I stopped him, reminding him that we had been traveling all day and I had a poop attack. He laughed and moved his lips back up to my lips before penetrating my pussy. I embraced each thrust and as he moved faster, my pussy got tighter.

While Ben was working his cock to make me wet, we heard a little voice that said, "Uncle

Ben, don't smush Audrey."

Ben stopped and looked at me with wide eyes. Carly had walked into the pool house and he didn't know what to do. He slowly moved off of me covering us both with the blanket. He asked, "Carly, what are you doing in here? Shouldn't you be in bed?"

Carly said, "Audrey said we could watch *The Wizard of Oz*."

Ben looked over at me with a look of wonder on how he should handle this predicament. I said, "Carly, of course we can watch *The Wizard of Oz*, but don't you think you should wear your red Dorothy shoes when we watch it?"

Carly said, "My mom says I can't wear shoes in bed."

Trying to find a way to get her to leave the pool house for a few minutes, I said, "Uncle Ben and I won't tell your mom if you wear them in our bed. Go get your red shoes and we will put on the movie *The Wizard of Oz*."

Carly said as she was leaving the pool house, "Okay, Audrey, I'll go get them."

The moment Carly left the pool house Ben and I jumped out of bed and put our pajamas on. I had a tank top and shorts while Ben had cotton pants and a t-shirt. We were dressed and back in bed by the time Carly came back into the pool house. Once she was back she jumped into bed with us handing Ben the DVD of *The Wizard of Oz*. Ben put it in the DVD player and then the three of us cuddled in the bed with Carly between us. A few minutes into the movie, I realized my surroundings. Here I was cuddled in bed with a five year old and a great man. I had never really thought about having children, I wanted them eventually, but at this moment I was in love with the idea. I whispered to Ben, "Is this what our life is going to be like with children?"

Ben kissed me on the forehead before whispering back, "Isn't it amazing?"

At that moment, I knew that Carly had played a major role in Ben's decision to move on from New York City playboy to a man who was ready to settle down. I guess I finally felt what most of my Facebook friends from high school were already experiencing. I cuddled into Ben and let Carly get more settled into me.

Not long into the movie, Carly fell asleep and not much longer after, I felt myself fall asleep. In the morning, I was the first to wake up. I woke up still cuddled up to Ben and Carly was sprawled out on the other side of him. My heart felt warm when I opened my eyes and saw them. It was a picture perfect moment. I had to pee really bad so I quietly snuck out of the bed and went to the bathroom. After I peed, I walked out of the pool house and into the house to get some juice. As I was walking into the kitchen, I heard Ben's mother and sister talking. I stopped when I heard my name to listen. His sister was going on about how she couldn't believe Ben would want to marry a girl like me and that she was sure I was only marrying him for his money. Ben's mother, Sherry defended me stating that she was sure I had made millions off my book *Dating Chase Walker*, but his sister said that making money off a relationship with a crazy man was wrong.

I stood and listened for a few minutes feeling completely offended, but knew that I did love Ben so I had to get his sister to see that. I could understand why people would think of me in a negative way because I wrote about sex. After listening to a lot of harsh words, I walked into the kitchen and said, "Good morning."

Sherry said, "Good morning, Audrey. How did you sleep?"

I said, "I slept great. Ben and Carly are still sleeping."

Catherine said, "Did Carly crawl into bed with you two last night?"

I said, "Yes, we watched *The Wizard of Oz* for about fifteen minutes before we fell asleep."

Catherine said, "Carly is obsessed with that movie. I'm sorry if she was a bother."

I said, "Oh, no, she wasn't a bother at all. We had fun."

Catherine asked if I wanted some coffee and I accepted before sitting down at the counter and joining the conversation. After overhearing them, I had a lot of sucking up to do. I did love Ben and loving him made me want his family to love me.

TIME FOR AUDREY BUCHANAN

Ben and I left California with me feeling like I had made a little progress getting his mother and sister to like me. His niece Carly and his brother-in-law Bo were in the bag. We arrived in Chicago and took a limo to my apartment. After we arrived, we put our pajamas on and jumped into bed. The cold made me miss California, but having Ben to cuddle with made it tolerable. We lay in my bed in silence for a few moments before I asked, "What happens next?"

Ben said, "Now we start trying to have a baby."

I moved out of our cuddle and asked, "What?"

Ben said, "I'm only kidding, but we can start practicing to make one."

I smiled as I said, "I'd be open to practicing," before I leaned in for a kiss.

Ben and I kissed for a few moments before he pulled the shirt off over my head. I then pulled his shirt off and told him how hot I thought he was. His face got a little red before he said, "You make me feel more confident in myself than anyone I know."

I said, "Good, now take your underwear off so I can put your cock in my mouth."

Ben awkwardly pulled his underwear off under the blanket and then I crawled under the covers and put his cock in my mouth. It had a little stench to it, but I didn't mind. I proceeded putting as much of it in my mouth as I could. From under the sheets I could hear Ben moaning and his moans turned me on. With his cock in my mouth and my right hand on his shaft to give him extra pleasure, I took my left hand and began to rub my pussy. Having his cock in my mouth and gently rubbing my clit made me get wet.

I kept moving his cock in and out of my mouth along with rubbing my clit for several minutes. Once I was wet, I crawled up and kissed Ben on the lips while I repositioned myself to sit on his hard cock. I slowly let it penetrate me and then moved my hips in a circular motion to get it settled inside my pussy. Once settled, I moved up and down slowly sending pleasure through my body.

I moved faster and faster and as I was riding Ben's cock, I used my left hand to rub my clit. I could feel the cum moving out of my pussy onto his cock and on my fingers. Feeling my cum made me more turned on and in order to prevent myself from coming right away, I moved my left hand up from rubbing my clit to grabbing my left boob. As I rubbed my breast, I felt the cum from my fingers rubbing on my breast. The cum made it easier for me to rub my breast and it felt good. I pulled on my nipple a little bit with my wet fingers and that got me. A few seconds later, my pussy began pulsating in orgasm. Ben came in the middle of my orgasm and his hard pulsating cock helped to prolong my orgasm.

After we both finished orgasming, I crash down on the bed and lay next to Ben. I closed my eyes taking in the sensation of the orgasm while I caught my breath. We didn't speak for several minutes until Ben pulled my body closed to his, kissed my forehead, and asked, "Now what?"

I said, "Now we go to sleep."

Ben laughed a little as he said, "'Now what?' means what are we going to do next? Are you going to come back to New York with me Tuesday?"

I said, "I'm not sure. I'll have to check my schedule to see what Steven has lined up for me. Do you want us to live in New York once we are married?"

Ben said, "I love New York, but technically I could live anywhere. I'd just have to travel to New York and London every few weeks."

I asked, "Do you want to live in Chicago?"

Ben said, "I can move to Chicago, but being back in the cold makes me think we should move to Southern California sooner rather than later. I enjoy the weather much better there."

I said, "I think we need to get your sister to like me before we go and move by her. How about we move out there in a few years?"

Ben said, "My sister likes you."

I said, "No, she thinks I'm after your money. I told you what I overheard her say when she didn't know I was in the kitchen."

Ben said, "She won't think that way once she has the opportunity to spend more time with you."

I dreaded spending more time with Ben's sister. Now his niece, Carly, I wish she was mine, which is strange because I don't like many children. Ben and I talked more about logistics and his biggest concern was living in my apartment if he moved to Chicago. He said he'd keep his condo in New York, but he thought we should purchase a new and bigger place in Chicago. When I asked what was wrong with my apartment, his arguments were that I didn't have a television or room for an office. I said to Ben, "It's time I make a confession.

Ben's eyes widened as he asked, "What kind of confession?"

I sat up and then got off the bed before I said, "Follow me." Ben hesitated as he got up from the bed, but took my hand as I led him to the other end of my apartment. When we got in front of a door, in which Ben had always thought was a closet, I said, "Open the door."

Ben looked confused, but opened the door. After the door was opened, he walked in and I turned on the light. Ben's jaw hit the ground before he said, "Oh, my God, I am marrying a hoarder."

I said, "I am not a hoarder."

Ben said, "Yes, yes, you are. Look at all of these boxes. This is crazy, Audrey. I can't believe I didn't know you had a second room in this apartment. What do you have in all of these boxes?"

I said, "Books. They are all full of books."

Ben asked, "Why do you have so many books in boxes?"

I said, "I like to read books and I thought one day I'd have a library in my house. I couldn't bear to give them up."

Ben said, "Alright, Audrey, I am going to buy you a house and that house is going to have a huge library for you to work. It will have enough shelves for all of your books."

I said, "Ben, just because we are getting married, it doesn't mean we need to buy a house in the suburbs."

Ben said, "Who said anything about a house in the suburbs?"

I said, "You said a house."

Ben said, "Okay, I'll be more specific and say a house in the city. Like a condo."

I said, "You own your place in New York so how about I buy our house here in Chicago and then if anything happens with us, we will each have our own places."

Ben said, "What do you mean 'happens with us?'"

I said, "You know if we decide not to get married or something. This has all been happening so fast."

Ben had a look of anguish on his face. I didn't mean to hurt him, but I was trying to be realistic. Everything between us was happening incredibly fast. Ben said, "I love you, Audrey, and I understand what you are saying, but I'm not going anywhere. Let's take a risk and build this life together," before he kissed me.

I felt the same way as Ben and I wanted to build a life together. I didn't want to spend another day without him, but I was scared. I knew I couldn't be scared anymore though. I was ready for real love so I kissed Ben back and then said with a smile, "Alright, but I've never bought a home before. I've only rented. Now that I have money I want to be part of the purchasing process. Whatever we buy together we go in fifty-fifty. Capiche? Our Chicago home is going to be OUR home. Together. We are going to pick it, build it and make it ours."

Ben said, "Got it. We will have a home where you will have a library and I will have an office with a television so I can watch sports."

I said, "That sounds perfect, darling," before giving Ben a kiss.

After our kiss, Ben asked, "Are you keeping any other secrets from me? Any other rooms full of things I need to know about?"

I said, "No, book collecting is it. Are you still going to marry me even though you think I'm a book hoarder?"

Ben said, "Nothing could stop me from marrying you."

The next morning I woke up and Ben was not next to me. I could hear him in my living room on the phone. I looked at the clock and it was 7am so I closed my eyes, rolled over and went back to sleep. It was much too early for me to be awake.

After sleeping for a couple more hours, I got out of bed before wandering into my bathroom to brush my teeth. I brushed my teeth and then walked out into the living room with no shirt on. I thought it would be sexy to walk out in the living room for Ben half naked. When I walked out of the room, Ben smiled at me so I proceeded toward him. When I got closer, I knelt down to pull his pants off and put his cock in my mouth. Ben held his hand over the receiver and said, "Not now," but I continued and put his cock in my mouth. Ben leaned back a little while he continued talking business into the phone and I slowly moved his cock in and out of my mouth. I felt it getting harder by the minute. I felt so turned on by knowing Ben was turned on. I kept my left hand on his shaft while I used my right hand to rub my clit.

I moved my mouth up and down on Ben's

cock using my left hand to give his entire cock pleasure. As Ben's cock got harder my pussy got wet, I continued and once I was completely turned on, I took my mouth off Ben's cock and moved my body north so I could put Ben's cock in my pussy.

When I was on Ben's lap I went to kiss him, but he stopped me signaling that he was on the phone. A moment later Ben said into the phone, "Carl, I am going to have to call you back." Ben hung up the phone and then threw it to the side before kissing me passionately. After a few minutes of kissing he said, "You are so bad, Audrey."

I responded, "I know, but you love it."

Ben said, "I do, but how am I going to make us money if we are having sex all the time?"

I said, "You can call Carl back in a few minutes and make some money."

Ben kissed me again while I slowly penetrated his cock into my pussy. It felt amazing. I loved having his cock inside of me. I moved slowly up and down for a few moments, enjoying each thrust. After my pussy made his cock good and wet, Ben grabbed my body and took control. He lay me down on my back while his cock was still inside my pussy. Once I was fully on my back, he slowly moved in and out of my pussy deep with control. I liked seeing the controlling side of Ben and it turned me on.

He continued moving in and out of me,

gradually increasing his pace. I closed my eyes and enjoyed each thrust. He grabbed the back of my neck and lifted my head a little bit to kiss me. After our kiss, he kept his face close to mine while he continued humping me. I don't know why, but the way his body looked while he was fucking me with his face down by mine made him look like a gargoyle. It was unattractive and started turning me off. I used my hands to guide his body up as I said, "Let me see your sexy body."

Ben smiled at me and I could tell he was flexing his stomach a little when he leaned back. That was much better. I took in each thrust and then Ben said, "You are a bad girl for making me stop working to fuck you."

I was taken aback at Ben's sudden dirty talk, but I liked it. I said, "You like when I'm bad."

Ben said, "Only a very bad girl takes me away from making money."

His words made me think for a moment. A man who would say something like that, especially during sex, had to be obsessed with making money. Men revealed their deepest darkest secrets during sex or while drunk. That was the moment I knew his vice. I decided to say, "I'm going to marry you and spend all your money."

Ben said, "How much of my money are you going to spend, bitch?"

Was this really happening? Was I really

talking dirty about money to turn Ben on? I knew he was turned on by it because I could feel his cock getting harder in my pussy. I said, "I'm going to spend ten thousand dollars."

Ben slowed down for a moment and sort of whispered, "Only ten thousand dollars? Come on, spend more than that."

I yelled out, "I'm going to spend six million dollars!"

Ben said, "Oh yeah, you want to spend that kind of money."

I said, "I'm going to spend all your fucking money."

Ben yelled out, "Fuck!" and I felt him cum inside of me. I was no longer turned on because my mind was trying to figure out this sexual money talk. I needed to figure out how I was going to be able to handle this kind of talk better in the future so I didn't lose my clit boner trying to keep up.

Ben caught his breath and said, "Sorry I came so fast. Money turns me on."

I said, "I caught on to that. I guess now I know your weakness."

Ben said, "You are my weakness, darling," before kissing my forehead.

I said, "I think money comes first though. Why do you love money so much?"

Ben said, "There's a satisfaction in having it, knowing I have the ability to go out and get whatever I desire."

I said, "Except me. I can't be bought."

Ben said, "Except you."

I asked, "Why did you want me to tell you I spent all your money while we were fucking?"

Ben responded, "Another sense of satisfaction is knowing I can provide for you enough to buy anything your heart desires."

I asked, "Let me get this straight, someone spending your money turns you on?"

Ben said, "You are making me sound like a crazy man."

I said, "Not at all. I'm just trying to understand this correctly because I want to be able to turn you on."

Ben said, "I wouldn't want just anyone spending my money. I love you so that makes me want to take care of you and give you the world. Money can do that."

I said, "Money helps, but I'm not marrying you for your money. I'm going to be a bajillionaire, remember?"

Ben said, "That's why I'm marrying you."

I asked, "You are marrying me for my money?"

Ben laughed as he said, "No, not your money."

Offended, I asked, "Why not? Is my money not good enough?"

Ben continued laughing and said, "Your money is amazing. Want me to triple it for you?"

I asked, "Can I trust you with my money?" Ben gave me a look, making me wish I could take back what I had just said. Wanting to repair the hurt I saw in Ben's eyes I said, "Alright, you can play with my money after we are married."

Ben lit up with excitement. It's possible his cock was getting hard again over our money talk, but I was exhausted. I think that everything that had happened over the past couple of weeks was catching up with me. My mind and body felt drained, so drained that I didn't even feel like I could write I was so exhausted. This was not a norm for me as I usually wrote my best stories during sleepless nights.

I went into my room and curled up in bed. I considered masturbating since my pussy was still wet from my sexual tease session with Ben, but I was too tired to masturbate. A few hours later, Ben woke me up with a kiss on my forehead. I smiled even before I opened my eyes. Once I did open my eyes, I saw Ben smiling back at me. I pulled him into bed with me and snuggled up to him. He smelled so good. He had showered, which was something I badly needed to do. Ben said to me, "Let's go out for dinner. I leave tomorrow and we've been cooped up in this apartment all day."

I said, "Ben, you are going to have to get used to a lazy ass like me. Being cooped up in an apartment all day is generally when I am doing some of my best writing."

Ben said, "You haven't written a word all

day."

I said, "I was brainstorming."

Ben said, "Sure you were. Take a shower so we can go to dinner. I'm starving."

T he next day Ben headed back to New York and I was back to doing local book signings and small interviews. The hype of my book had died down and I was secretly grateful. The past few months had caught up with me, making my body feel more tired than ever before. So much had changed in my life in such a short period of time that I needed to let my body catch up to the changes.

I went to the book signings and interviews, but went straight home after each one. Even Steven said I didn't seem like myself, but he still had big plans for me. Bravo TV was casting a new reality show about Chicago social lives and he thought I was a perfect fit with my millionaire fiancé. Steven mentioning the words "reality show" made me feel uneasy. It made me think about Chase and how badly he was chasing the reality show dream.

Ben wouldn't be coming back to Chicago on Saturday because he had to meet with one of his investing partners, Sal. He said he had to seal a big deal that was going to change our lives. My life was changing with each day that passed. I missed Ben, but I was sort of glad because I still felt so exhausted. Nikki knew how exhausted I had been feeling so she booked a spa day for us at the Russian spa and bathhouse, Red Square. I couldn't wait to spend the day relaxing.

When we arrived at the bathhouse, it was empty. We were the only ones there with the staff, which was completely abnormal for the Chicago hotspot. As we checked in, the staff knew all of our names and welcomed us with champagne. Nikki said to the woman behind the desk, "I can't believe how empty it is in here. Are there a lot of people downstairs in the sauna and hot tub?"

The woman answered in a Russian accent, "No, the whole facility is yours for the day compliments of Mr. Benjamin Wright. Whatever you need, just ask."

Nikki said, "Holy shit, Ben rented this fucking place out for the day. How much money does he have, Audrey?"

I said, "I don't know. A lot, I guess."

Bree asked, "Haven't you guys talked about finances since you are getting married?"

I led the way downstairs to the locker room as I said, "No, it's his money, but we are going fifty-fifty on buying a new home in Chicago."

Bree said, "Yeah, but when you get married, it will be your money, too."

I said, "I have plenty of money, but it sure is fun dating a rich guy who likes to spend his money."

Nikki said, "Yeah, what the fuck? You've dated two totally rich guys that bought you everything."

Bree said, "Not really. I shouldn't bring up his name, but Chase's car was just repossessed and the owner is trying to evict him from his place at the Trump."

I asked, "What? Chase said he owned his place."

Bree said, "No, one of his client's owns it and let him move in there, but Chase hasn't paid rent in over six months now."

I said, "Chase told me he owned the place. I am confused. He wasn't paying his rent while I was with him? How the hell was he buying me all those gifts?"

Bree said, "I guess he was using credit cards because word on the street is that he's completely broke."

Nikki asked, "Didn't Chase just get money from your movie deal?"

I said, "Not yet. The movie deal check won't come through for a little while. That's so strange that he's broke. We broke up like four months ago and he was spending money like it was nothing."

Bree said, "Scotty said he didn't really even have that much to begin with and that the production company that he hired to follow him around for the reality show pilot is suing him for almost two-hundred thousand dollars that he never paid them."

I said, "Ouch. Let's not talk about Chase anymore." To change the subject I asked, "Nikki, who is your latest fling?"

Nikki told us all about her latest fling and we chatted about girlie things in the hot tub and sauna for the next hour until we were called upstairs for our massages and facials. After our massages, we got manicures and pedicures and I felt so refreshed. We had the place to ourselves all day so we stayed in our robes and sat at the bar. After several glasses of champagne I said, "I can't believe I am getting married."

Drunk too, Bree answered, "No shit. I can't believe you are getting married before me!"

Nikki's jaw and my jaw dropped when we heard Bree swear. Bree never swore. I said, "I never thought I'd get married before you either, Bree."

Bree said, "It just isn't fair. Scotty and I have been dating forever and you and Ben have known each other for a hot second."

Nikki laughed as she said, "To be fair, they met like six years ago and they have been Facebook friends since."

Bree drunkenly slurred as she said, "I'm sorry I'm being bitter. I am really happy for you, Audrey."

I said, "I know. I don't have to get married for a long time. We can wait if you want. I'm not in any rush. I'm not even sure why we are already engaged."

Bree said, "Because you are in love."

When I heard Bree say that, I felt a happiness run through my body that I had never felt before and I smiled. I said, "I am. I really am."

Bree said, "I love seeing you happy with a good man, Audrey. I promise no more bitterness. Let's start planning your wedding!"

I said, "My wedding will be easy. I just need to pick out a destination and a dress."

Bree said, "You still need to plan it."

I said, "Nope, resorts have packages and planners for this. I'll let Ben pick the date and then the planner can take over."

Nikki said, "You are so strange. Every girl wants to plan their wedding."

I said, "Not me. The perfect wedding for me is not having to plan a thing. The only thing I want to do is pick out my dress because I already have an idea of what I want in my head. None of the other nonsense matters as long as Ben and I are there."

I got home from our relaxing day and cuddled up in bed before calling Ben to thank him for renting out the entire spa for us for the day. I was feeling relaxed and rejuvenated, which made me excited that I'd see Ben the next night. Ben and I talked for awhile and he told me he wanted to show me a surprise the moment he got to Chicago the next day so he would be sending a car to pick me up in the afternoon. I told him he had surprised me enough, but he said it was our engagement gift. I didn't know what surprise he had up his sleeve, but I had never been disappointed with one of his surprises before so I was excited.

The next morning I woke up early for a meeting with my agent. I was feeling much better, but still made myself a large cup of coffee. When I arrived at my agent's office, Steven was there and the first thing that crossed my mind was that I was about to be tag teamed by Steven and my agent for not wanting to do any more promotions. My agent's assistant walked us into my agent's office and Steven and I sat down. I asked, "What's this meeting about?"

My agent asked, "What's next, Audrey?"

I asked, "What's next with what?"

Steven said, "You haven't been keen on doing appearances and promotions anymore so is my job here done?"

I asked, "Aren't my fifteen minutes of fame over? Can I just spend time resting and relaxing now?"

Steven said, "If you want to keep selling, and you do want a hype because of your movie deal, you need to keep up with promotions."

I said, "I'd rather just be writing and..." I tried to think of an excuse for a moment and decided to say, "I have a wedding to plan."

My agent asked, "Is your wedding more important than your writing career?"

I said, "No, I am still writing. I just don't

understand why I have to keep doing all these interviews? Aren't I old news now? Plus, Chase is out there doing interviews so that should keep my sales up."

My agent said, "Yes, Chase's ridiculous interviews about him thinking he's God are helping your sales, but we need to keep you in the limelight too. What new writing have you done?"

I said, "I sent you my most recent story about Tonya, the small town girl who moved to New York City and slept her way up to fame."

My agent said, "Yeah, I liked it, but we need something better now that you've set the bar so high. What else do you have? Do you have any more emotional memoirs on your hands? We could do a whole series following your love life."

I immediately thought about the last story I wrote when Ben didn't show up at the Empire State Building, but I knew in my head that needed to be deleted. I didn't want Ben finding out the sexual mishaps I had after my breakup with Chase. I said, "Umm, no."

My agent said, "Let me read it."

I asked, "Read what?"

My agent said, "Let me read whatever story you are hiding from me."

I said, "I am not hiding anything."

My agent said, "I've been working with you for years now, Audrey, and you always look down and clench your fists when you lie. What story did you write that you don't want to share?"

I said, "Nothing. If I had more time, I could write something."

My agent said, "No, you have something. What is it?"

I said, "It was just another nonsense continuation of my life after Chase. It's total crap."

My agent's eyes opened wide and she smiled as she said, "That's perfect! Another memoir. It could be like a book reality series. Send it to me as soon as possible."

I said, "I can't because it's too personal and I don't want Ben reading it."

Steven said, "I love it! A reality book series. I can promote that easily and it could lead into another movie deal. Let us read it."

I said, "No."

My agent said, "Yes."

I said, "No."

My agent said, "Yes, Audrey. I expect you to email it to me tonight."

I stood up as I said, "No, I'm happy and I am in love with a great guy. I am not going to ruin it by exposing the ridiculous sex I had with other people when Ben was trying to date me."

I started walking out when my agent said, "Just send it to me so I can read it. I love reading your writing. You can decide if we publish it."

As I exited the door I turned around and said, "Fine, but only if Steven promises no more interviews with TV, radio, or newspapers for a month. Only book signings."

My agent simply replied, "Send me the story, Audrey."

I got home after the meeting and sat down at my computer. I stared at my home screen for a few minutes and then opened a document I had titled *Time for Me*. I started reading it and as I read it, I hated the emotion it brought to me. That feeling I felt after Chase left me to pursue multiple women. That feeling of when I shit my pants. That feeling of wasting my time on a man who created a façade and I fell for it. I read on, though, and I felt myself smiling recalling the moment when Ben first messaged me and the conversation we had when he convinced me to come to New York for a weekend. I kept on reading, skipping all the parts not involving Ben and I felt a new kind of happiness inside of me. There was so much kindness and love in this story. As I read my words, I could feel my love for Ben warming my insides and I wanted to kick myself for not realizing it sooner. I was so lucky he didn't know all the nonsense I had participated in and it made me nervous for him to find out because it might scare him off. I didn't want him to walk away from me because of it, but the thought that I should be honest with him did cross my mind. Handing him this story to read would put it all on the table so he'd know and there'd be no secrets between us, on my side at least.

I wasn't sure if I was going to send the story on to my agent, but something inside of me started telling me I should share it with Ben to let him know the whole truth. I always shared my feelings best through the written word and him reading this story would share not only my sexual mishaps with Ben, but it would also be an opportunity for me to show him how my love was true.

I got lost in a stare thinking about what I should do when I heard my phone ring. I saw it was Ben and a smile grew on my face. I answered, "Hello."

Ben asked, "How was the meeting with your agent this morning?"

I said, "I am taking a month off from most promotions. I only have to do book signings."

Ben said, "That's great. Now you will have time to plan our wedding."

I said, "Ben, I have a confession."

Ben asked, "Uh oh, what's your confession?"

I said, "I don't want to plan our wedding."

Ben sounded like he had some nervousness in his voice when he asked, "What are you saying, Audrey?"

I said, "No, oh no, please don't take that the wrong way. I want to get married! I can't wait to marry you, but I wasn't kidding when I said I didn't want to have to deal with planning a wedding. I just want to fly out to some resort and get married on the beach. Can we just elope?"

Ben said, "We can do whatever you want. I would like my family there though. Don't you want your family there?"

I said, "Yes, I do, but I don't want to plan anything. The only thing I want to pick out is my dress."

Ben said, "I'll hire a wedding planner, but I have to go because my flight is about to take off. Remember, the driver is picking you up in an about an hour. Will you wear a sexy black dress for me? Oh, and bring an overnight bag."

I said, "Yes, sir. I'll get ready now."

"I love you, Audrey."

"I love you too, Ben."

I hung up the phone and read my story for a little while longer before going into my bedroom to pack an overnight bag. While I was packing, I realized I had to take a shit and I was a little pissed because I had showered earlier and I was ready to get laid when I saw Ben. Even with "no wipers" I still worried something might be left down there. I especially didn't like a guy going down on me after dropping a deuce. I took a quick body shower to wash my ass crack and do a quick shave. I couldn't wait to have sex. I hoped Ben had booked us a room at some sexy hotel for the night because I wanted sex and once my ass crack was clean and fresh I was feeling extra sexy.

The limo driver called when he was in front of my building and I walked downstairs. Of course there was a bottle of champagne waiting for me in the back of the limousine with a note from Ben that read, "Our lives are going to go so many wonderful places together. I can't wait to take this journey with you, my bride."

I smiled as I put Ben's note down and poured myself a glass of champagne. I was living every girl's dream and I am not sure how a girl like me was able to score such an amazing man. Maybe sharing my most recent story, *Time for Me*, was not a good idea because I didn't want to risk losing such an incredible man. I needed more time to think about letting Ben, and the world, have access to more of my intimate words.

The driver arrived at O'Hare Airport and pulled into an area I wasn't familiar with. I looked out the window wondering how he was able to pull out so close to the runway. We kept driving when we pulled up near a private jet. My face moved close to the window while I chugged the rest of my glass of champagne. As I looked out the window, I saw Ben walk out of a jet before the driver opened my door. I stepped out of the limo and smiled at Ben before I ran toward him and he ran down the stairs to meet me. Ben wrapped his arms around me before he gave me a big kiss. I asked, "Did you take a private jet here?"

Ben said, "Audrey, this is our jet."

My eyes widened when I asked, "What?"

Ben said, "This is our very own jet. We can

take it wherever we want, whenever we want."
I was in shock. Had Ben really just purchased an airplane? I stood silent looking at Ben, then the airplane, then back to Ben, and then the airplane again. Ben continued asking, "Do you like it?" I didn't respond. I was still in shock and in my mind I kept thinking how I was about to marry a man who just bought a fucking airplane. Ben said, "I'm so sorry. I should've talked with you about this before I bought it. We are a team now and we should make decisions together."

I finally formed words in my mouth and said, "No, no, it's your money. I'm just in shock that I'm dating a man who owns an airplane."

Ben said, "You are marrying a man who you own an airplane with. This is our airplane."

I shook my head back and forth with a smile as I said, "I love it and you never have to ask me if you can spend your money on something, unless it's a stripper. No strippers or hookers, but everything else is fair game."

Ben laughed a little and said, "Audrey, my money is our money now and we are a team so from now on I will talk to you before I buy an airplane."

I said, "This is crazy!"

Ben said, "I've always wanted an excuse to buy a jet and now I have once since I'll need to travel more living in Chicago."

I smiled before Ben gave me a kiss. We then walked onto the jet, a jet that apparently I fucking owned. My mom was going to go crazy over this one. I couldn't believe it. Ben and I took a quick selfie photo and then I posted it on my social media. Flying on and owning a private jet was something I absolutely had to brag about. After posting the photo, Ben said we were going to fly back to New York for dinner and then stay the night there. He had a meeting in the morning and then we could head back to Chicago to start looking for a new home.

After the flight took off, I gave Ben a look like I was so smitten and smiled at him. He smiled back and as he smiled, I unbuckled my seatbelt before getting up and straddling him. He unbuckled his belt and put his right hand on my cheek as he kissed me. I kissed him back using my right hand to rub his cock from over his pants. I felt his cock getting harder with each movement I made. Ben used his left hand to unzip my dress and then took his right hand off my face to pull my dress down. My bare breasts were out and soon his lips moved away from my lips and were on my nipples. I looked down as I watched him kiss and caress my breasts. He looked so sexy to me. Partly because he had a smoking hot face and body, partly he made me feel so much happiness inside, and partly because he had just bought us a fucking airplane. I could feel myself getting wet. My nipples got hard with each motion and when Ben looked up at me with a smile I was ready to feel him inside of me.

I bit my lip and said, "Fuck me."

Ben used his strong arms to lift me off his lap before standing up to take his pants off. As I pulled my dress and panties off, Ben said, "My God, you are beautiful. You are perfection. I am the luckiest man in the world."

I smiled as I said, "I'm the luckiest girl. Now turn me around and fuck me on your airplane, Mr. Wright."

Ben used a little force as he turned me around and bent me over the seat before he penetrated my pussy from behind. I moaned in pleasure as his cock entered my wet pussy. I loved having him inside of me. Ben moved with slow motions in and out of my pussy at first, but then moved faster. As Ben was holding my hips and moving in and out of my pussy he said, "Your ass is amazing, baby, I mean darling," before he spanked me.

I said, "Spank me again," and he did.

Ben having control was such a turn on. I loved feeling him holding my hips and moving his cock in and out of my pussy. I loved feeling his strength. I loved him spanking me and making me feel like I had been bad. Ben pulled his cock out of my pussy and then with force led me to the bench where he pushed me down before penetrating my pussy again. Once inside of me, he used his thumb to rub my clit. He was sending double the pleasure through my body. I looked at him with my feet wrapped around his head and smiled before closing my eyes to take in the pleasure. I could feel my pussy tightening just from feeling his control. Ben whispered, "Yeah, tighten that wet pussy for me."

I kept embracing the pleasure and with each thrust, my pussy got tighter and tighter until it was so tight I had to release an orgasm. As I let go and orgasmed, I could feel Ben orgasm, too. His pulsating cock heightened my orgasm even more. After our bodies were both finished releasing a massive amount of pleasure, Ben crashed down on me to catch his breath which had become heavy. We relaxed for several moments before he rolled off of me and we sat up. Still naked, Ben asked, "More champagne, my dear?"

I said, "But of course."

We drank our champagne in the buff until our glasses were empty and then put our clothes back on. When we landed in New York, there was a car there ready to take us to dinner. As I walked out of our private jet, I felt like I was living in a movie or a really good book. Never did I imagine my life to be moving in this direction. Just over a year ago, I was barely making rent, but now I owned half of a fucking airplane. My life had done a complete one eighty and I had never felt happier.

After dinner, we got to Ben's condo and I had never felt so tired in my life. My body actually ached and for some odd reason my right boob was really sore. I wasn't expecting my period to come anytime soon and I didn't remember Ben being rough with my breasts while we fucked on the jet, but it was possible he had been so I tried to ignore it. As we cuddled up in bed, I was ready to fall asleep after a day of traveling, fucking, and eating massive amounts of food at dinner, but Ben gave me the "I want to fuck" look so I leaned in and kissed him. He kissed me back as he moved on top of me. He moved quick as he pulled my pants off and then pulled his pants off before penetrating me.

I was enjoying it, but not totally into it because my body felt so exhausted. I wanted to close my eyes and enjoy the pleasure of his cock moving in and out of my pussy, but I was afraid if I closed my eyes I'd fall asleep. I decided to push Ben off of me and get on all fours knowing that Ben came faster when we fucked doggie style. As he was penetrating me from behind, I pulled my shirt off and all I could think about was how tender my right boob felt. I tried to ignore it and get my mind to think about the pleasure Ben was creating in my pussy, but once I stopped thinking about my tender breast I felt a sneeze coming on. I squinted my eyes and tried to hold back the sneeze, but I couldn't hold it back and sneezed. My sneeze must've caused my pussy to tighten because after I sneezed I felt Ben cum inside of me. Another sneeze came on, but once you sneeze once it is impossible to hold back the second one so I sneezed again. I thought I was finished sneezing, but a third one came on and when I sneezed for the third time a fart snuck out of my ass and my jaw dropped in embarrassment. Ben fell over and started laughing. He said, "I just felt a fart come out of your butt!"

I felt my face turn red in embarrassment and said, "Oh, my God, I'm so sorry."

Ben continued laughing. He was lying on the bed, almost kicking he was laughing so hard. I looked at him totally embarrassed before he said, "Don't be embarrassed."

I said, "I just farted on you when you were orgasming."

Ben was still laughing while he said, "I'm sorry I can't stop laughing."

Watching Ben laugh into tears made me start laughing, too. I was embarrassed, but it was funny so I got over the embarrassment and enjoyed the humor of the situation. We laughed a little longer and then I curled up in Ben's arms. Once comfortable, Ben said, "Don't fart on me again." I gave Ben a little smack from over my shoulder and then he said, "I'm only kidding. I love you. Good night, darling."

As I closed my eyes I said, "I love you, too."

I felt Ben kiss the back of my neck and moments later I was asleep.

Ben and I got back to Chicago and started house hunting. Ben wanted to live in a high rise, but I was working on getting him to fall in love with an old warehouse I had found in the West Loop. He kept saying he'd feel more comfortable knowing I was in a secure building with a doorman. After a couple days of nagging I was able to convince him that the old warehouse was the place for us and the next day we signed a contract buying out the entire building. The day after that we met with a contractor who would be building to the specifications of our dream home.

After we left the meeting with the contractor, Ben said it was time for us to buy a car. I told him how I had planned on buying a fancy car when I made a lot of money and I was waiting for my movie deal check to come in so I could buy it. He told me we didn't need to wait for my check and we should get a car for us now. I explained there was no indoor parking at the apartment I lived in now so we should wait until we moved into our new place before we got a car. He agreed that was probably best.

On our cab ride home from the contractor

meeting, my agent called. I answered it saying, "Hello."

My agent said, "It's been two weeks, Audrey. When are you going to send me that story?"

I said, "I don't know if I am going to send it."

My agent said, "Send it. You can decide later if you want to publish it."

I said, "I don't even know if I want you to read it. Let me think about it one more night and I'll call you tomorrow."

My agent said, "Call me first thing in the morning or I'll be calling you."

I said, "Okay."

"Goodbye, Audrey."

I said, "I'll talk to you tomorrow," before I hung up the phone.

I put my phone back in my purse and Ben asked, "Who don't you want to read what?"

I said, "Nice eavesdropping."

Ben said, "Sorry."

I said, "I wrote this story, but I'm not sure I want to get published."

Ben asked, "You know, I've been meaning to ask you if you've ever written about me?"

I nervously said, "Well, err umm, this story is actually about you. I mean, it involves you."

Ben asked, "Really?"

I said, "Yeah, well, it is more like journaling and it is the story of what happened right after Chase broke up with me. It goes all the way until the night I was supposed to meet you at the Empire State Building."

Ben asked, "When did you write it?"

I said, "I wrote it in the hotel room in New York when I locked myself in there after you didn't show up at the Empire State Building. I was sad and writing is the way I get my emotions out."

Ben kissed my forehead and said he was sorry that he wasn't there, but would've been if he wasn't given the wrong date in the note sent to him. I told him I knew that now, but at the time I had been full of emotion, thinking I had realized my love for him too late. Ben then asked if he could read the story and I told him I was scared to let him read it because it exposed me hooking up with other people while he and I were talking. He said reading my book *Dating Chase Walker* was hard, but reading it didn't make him love me any less. I explained to him how it was different because he and I were talking when I had hooked up with other people and that's when he confessed that he had hooked up with a woman right before Christmas. When he told me he had had sex with another woman I felt a sting hit my heart, but I couldn't be mad because at that same time I was off munching some random girl's rug in Los Angeles and hooking up with a guy I only knew as 'G.' I said, "I don't like hearing that. It hurts."

Ben said, "I'm sorry. I didn't want to hurt

you by telling you that. You had pulled away from me and I didn't know if anything was going to come of us. You acted so distant that I didn't think you wanted to be with me. I didn't even enjoy myself while I was with her because I kept thinking about you. In all my years of screwing around with women I have never thought of another woman while I was with a different woman. That doesn't count for threesomes because I had to do double duty. Oh, and there was this one girl I picked up when I was wasted. I must've been blacked out and all of the sudden I woke up to her riding me and if I didn't think of another woman, my dick would have gone soft. See, I've been around the block, too. It's our past and somehow in a twisted way those sexual adventures brought us to where we are right now, together."

The cab pulled in front of my building and as Ben paid the cab driver, I smiled at Ben and gave him a quick kiss before I asked, "How the fuck did I get so lucky to find you?"

Ben said, "Hey now, I found you on that yacht. Don't take credit for my find."

I laughed as I got out of the cab and as we walked up the stairs I said, "I am still scared to let you read the story. I want you to read about the love I have for you, but nothing else."

Ben said, "I'll leave it up to you, but know that I'd love nothing more than to read your words of passion for me."

A couple days passed and we acted like an

old married couple, spending our time picking out tile, wood, appliances and other random shit for our new home. On the morning Ben was leaving, I woke up while he was in the shower. I pulled my computer off the nightstand and sent him my story titled *Time for Me*. I decided that even though I was scared for him to read about my sexual mishaps, I was about to marry this man and I couldn't go into a marriage with any secrets. I also wanted him to be able to read the words I had written that led me to falling in love with him.

After I pressed send on the email, I got out of bed and walked into the bathroom. I wanted to join him in the shower for a quick fuck before he would be gone for the next two days. I walked into the bathroom and it smelled like shit. I plugged my nose and loudly said, "Pee yew!"

Ben stopped his singing, peeked his head out from behind the shower curtain, and said. "Sorry, I just took a huge dump."

I said, "Oh my God Ben, your shit stinks. I was going to join you in the shower, but I don't think I'll be able to breathe in here."

Ben said, "Get in here, hottie. The soap makes it smell much better behind the curtain."

I threw off my t-shirt and jumped in the shower with Ben. He put a large amount of soap on the loofah trying to make the flowery scent cover the stench from his poop. He took the loofah and rubbed it over my body. As he was scrubbing my back with his left hand, I could feel his right hand gently moving down my back, past my crack and onto my pussy. He rubbed my labia slowly before inserting his finger inside my pussy. The combination of him moving his finger in and out slowly along with the bubbles running down my back and over my pussy sent chills through my body.

I took in the pleasure as I felt my pussy get more and more wet. Ben whispered in my ear from behind, "I love feeling your cum on my fingers."

I smiled a little and then got back to concentrating on the pleasure Ben's hands were creating inside of my body. As he was moving his finger in and out of my pussy, I felt him slip his hard cock inside of me. I moaned in pleasure, feeling the difference in girth entering my pussy. I bent over slightly, making it easier for him to penetrate me from behind while I put my hands on the shower wall for balance. Ben continued moving in and out of my pussy while bubbles grew all over my body from the soap on the loofah. I took each moment of penetration in and enjoyed the slow increase in speed, which made my pussy tighten up.

Once my pussy was tightly hugging Ben's cock he said, "I am going to cum" so I concentrated as hard as I could before releasing the tension in my pussy, creating a light orgasm to flow through my body. As my body was slightly twitching from the release of my orgasm, I felt Ben's cock begin pulsating inside of my pussy in orgasm. Once both our orgasms finished taking over our bodies and we were completely relaxed, Ben said, "I love you so much."

I smiled before I said, "I love you, too."

Ben kissed the back of my head before getting out, stating he was too hot to be in the shower anymore. I washed my hair and then got out of the shower. When I walked out of the bathroom, Ben was getting dressed. I crawled onto the bed wearing a robe and said, "I have a surprise for you."

Ben asked, "Really?"

I said, "Yes, I emailed it to you this morning. If you read it and never want to come back to me, I will understand."

Ben stopped what he was doing, came over to me, kissed me, and said, "I'm so glad you decided to let me read your story and nothing, nothing could ever stop me from loving you, Audrey."

I smiled at Ben. His words had spread happiness through my body and all I wanted to do was pull him close to me. I wanted to hug him tight, so I did. I wrapped my arms around him and pulled him down onto the bed with me before I said, "Stay. Don't go to New York for the day. I don't want you to leave."

Ben said, "I don't want to go, but I have to. Don't worry, I am working on getting everything settled so I don't have to leave as much. I'll be on my way back as soon as I can tomorrow."

I said, "Okay, Mr. Wright."

Ben said, "You can always come with me, Mrs. Wright."

I said, "I wish I could, but I have a damn book signing tomorrow morning and Nikki is coming over tonight to help me look online for things for our new home!"

Ben got up out of bed and then handed me his credit card, telling me to buy whatever I wanted before he headed out the door. I stayed in bed. My body was still feeling tired, which was probably a result from all the Red Bull I had to drink over the past couple of days to get rid of the tiredness I was experiencing before. I pulled my computer off my nightstand and bounced around on Facebook for a little while before deciding to take a nap.

I woke up five hours later and put some clothes on before Nikki came over. I sent a text to Nikki asking her to pick up wine. I was excited to spend some time with Nikki and do some home shopping. The combination of my tiredness, the cold, and being in love was making me domesticated, I guess. While I was waiting for Nikki to arrive Ben sent me a text saying, "I love reading your story. It makes me feel like you are right here with me. I want to keep reading instead of going into this meeting."

I responded back with a smile emojicon. I

was glad Ben was enjoying my story, but still scared of what he would think when he got to the parts where I acted like a complete whore. After I sent the smiley emojicon there was a knock on the door. I figured it was Nikki so I walked over and opened the door. When I opened the door Chase was standing on the other side. I didn't say a thing. I slammed the door shut in his face, but he stopped it with his foot and let himself in. I said, "Chase, come on now. Can't you just leave me alone?"

Chase said, "I need something from you."

I said, "Of course you do. Can't you use your spiritual powers to get whatever the fuck you need? Aren't you like a superhero now or something?"

Chase said, "No, what I need is the only thing my mind cannot provide me."

I said, "I am not sleeping with you."

Chase said, "My life is plentiful in sex."

I said, "That's fantastic. So the group relationship is working out for you?"

"Yes, but we are still waiting for you to join us on our spiritual and sexual journey."

"Get the fuck out of here. Why the hell would I ever want to get involved with your bizarre world?"

"Because you still love me and you are waiting for me. You will be mine again."

I said, "You are fucking nuts. I will never be yours again. I'm getting married to the most amazing man that ever existed."

Chase said, "No, you aren't. You won't marry him. I've seen the future."

I rolled my eyes at Chase before asking, "Why are you here, Chase? What the fuck do you need from me?"

Chase said, "I need you to give me the money owed to me now."

I said, "I haven't received any money from the movie yet. You will get your cut the same time I get mine."

Chase said, "I need it now."

I lied when I said, "I don't have that kind of money," although I had made well over a million in book sales already.

Chase said, "Audrey, I need this money now."

I asked, "Why? Don't you have plenty of money from your clients? You have a big house and fancy car so what else do you need to buy?

Chase fell to the ground in tears. I guess one thing didn't change about Chase and he still had his constant crying fits. I thought to myself: *Fuck, now I have to deal with a crying man*, but I dealt with his crying with compassion like I always had and sat down on the ground in front of Chase. He wept for a few more moments before he said, "There was never any money."

I said, "Never any money with what?"

Chase said, "I am broke. I never had any money. I started getting all this publicity with what I was doing and assumed the money would just come so I took out credit card after credit card and personal loans. I rented my place at Trump Tower from a client who I haven't paid in months. If I don't pay him this week, I'll be evicted and the production company I hired to film for me is threatening to sue me if I don't pay them in five business days."

I asked, "You are broke?"

Chase said, "I thought I was going to be pulling in tons of money. I made a bad call." He started crying harder and then continued, "You can help me. You owe me, Audrey!"

I said, "I owe you nothing, Chase. I gave you a fair amount in my movie deal."

"I deserve more money and you know it. Think about all the stuff I bought you."

"Are you really trying to get money back for things you bought me?"

"I was so good to you. It's your turn to be good to me."

"That's fucking ridiculous."

Chase looked up at me with his red teary eyes and said, "If I don't get this money now the girls will leave me and I'll have no shot at my reality show. Don't ruin everything for me."

"So let me get this straight, you want me to give you money so you can fund your ridiculous polygamous relationship?"

"I am the provider and link of the relationship. My women count on me to be their king."

I said, "You are a king without a kingdom. I think you need to reveal this to your women."

Chase said, "I won't be broke when you give me the money you owe me and my reality show will be picked up. My powers are unique and no network will be able to deny me."

I said, "Chase, there are already reality shows about polygamy out there and what you are doing is nothing new."

Chase said, "It is though. I have powers. You should see the barriers I've broken with these women."

I said, "Chase, you chose girls who will do anything to be famous. You didn't do anything except pick up a bunch of desperate girls."

Chase said, "Audrey, I wish you'd open your eyes up to see what I am doing. I am not worried though. You will come around and understand and when you do, we will welcome you into our spiritual circle of love with open arms."

I said, "Chase, you are a nut case. It's time for you to go."

Chase lay on the ground and started kicking and screaming like a spoiled child saying, "I'm not leaving without the money," over and over.

I quietly said, "Chase, come on now, get yourself together. You are acting like a child. It's time for you to leave."

He kept on crying and pounding his fists on the ground. I stood there, letting him throw his temper tantrum and while I was standing there waiting for him to exhaust himself and wishing I had a glass of wine and popcorn to go with this show of a lifetime, Nikki walked in the door. She looked at Chase on the ground and then looked at me before asking, "What the fuck is going on here?"

Chase immediately stopped his temper tantrum and crying. He then stood up and said to Nikki, "Audrey wasn't listening to me."

I said, "The fuck I wasn't! I was being nice and listening to you until you turned into a mother fucking child and threw a temper tantrum."

Nikki asked, "Seriously, what the fuck is going on? And why is he here?"

Chase said, "I'm here for my money and Audrey won't give it to me."

I said, "He's fucking broke so he needs me to front him the money he is getting for the movie."

Chase said, "It is my money. You took my identity and made a profit off of it. I created the man of Chase Walker and I should be reaping the benefits."

Nikki looked at me and I gave her the go ahead and go "Italian bitch" on him look. She smiled back at me before she walked over to Chase, grabbed his ear and pulled him out the door. As she was throwing him out she yelled, "Clean up your own mess, you fucking scrub!" She then slammed the door and locked it behind her. When she turned around after locking the door, she shook her head back and forth and asked, "What the fuck?"

I said, "I don't even know what to say."

Nikki said, "I told you from the beginning he was bad news for you, but you didn't listen."

I said, "He still thinks I am going to be with him in the future."

Nikki said, "He thinks that because you are too fucking nice to him. If I had dated him and he showed up at my house asking for money after we broke up, I'd kick him in the fucking balls. He needs a good kick in the balls. Maybe it will kick the wackadoodle out of his head and make him somewhat normal again."

I said, "I think he's just having an identity crisis. A cry for attention and he believes this will give him attention."

Nikki said, "He is looking for attention in all the wrong ways."

I said, "Let's open that bottle of wine!"

Nikki opened the wine and I picked up the phone to order food. After I ordered food, I sent Ben a text that said, "I love you" just because after I saw Chase I was reminded again of just how lucky I was to have Ben. Once I sent the text I said thinking out loud to Nikki, "What if Ben is broke too and it's all just a façade? What if I fell for another crazy man?

Nikki said, "I fucking told you Chase was disgusting when you first met him. Ben is different. He is real and he really loves you."

I asked, "Are you sure? I mean, Chase presented himself and I thought my love for him was real."

Nikki said, "There's a difference. Your love was real for Chase, but his love for you was and is not. Chase creates a façade of love for attention, for companionship because he cannot be alone, for his career, and to be worshiped. Ben? Well, Ben went out and earned what he wanted before really loving a woman. He found himself and satisfied his selfish needs before he found the one to love."

I said, "You make good points and you sound a little like Bree right now."

Nikki continued, "Trust me on this, Audrey, you are making a great decision by marrying Ben. He is good for you. He may not be a psychotic man that will make for a ridiculous story, but the story you write about him will be the story of your life. His impact on you won't be hot and cold drama, his impact on you will be everlasting true love."

I said, "Nikki, you are getting fucking deep here. Have you been drinking already?"

Nikki said, "No, I think about this kind of shit all the time and for some reason, I've been thinking about the whirlwind year you've had. I'm a little jealous of it actually."

I asked, "Why would you be jealous of me?"

Nikki said, "Because you finally found the wrong man and once you find the truly wrong man, you find the right man. It's simple math."

I said, "So Chase fucking with my head was part of my journey to find the right man who is Ben?"

Nikki said, "Yes, haven't you ever watched a romantic comedy? That's how it happens. I've found a lot of wrong men, but not a man wrong enough to lead me to the right man. Surely nobody as fucking crazy as Chase Walker."

I said, "He wasn't that crazy."

Nikki said, "Chase Walker is the definition of crazy."

I said, "Let's move on. I have a credit card with no limit and an entire house to decorate."

Nikki said, "Look at you, Suzie Homemaker. You have no idea how fucking lucky you are to have Ben."

I said, "I do know how lucky I am. It took me a couple months to realize it, but I know it now and I couldn't be happier."

When Ben got back to Chicago, I couldn't wait to see him. I missed him, which was strange because he was only gone a day. He arrived at my apartment and I jumped on him the moment he walked in the door. I kissed him and he said, "I have something to tell you."

I said, "Fuck me before you tell me."

He said, "I'm not going to argue with that."

Ben walked to my bedroom carrying me. My legs were wrapped around him as he walked and when he got into my bedroom, he threw me down on the bed. I pulled my shirt off over my head and then pulled down my pants while Ben did the same. Once we were both naked, Ben crawled on top of me and said, "You are so beautiful, perfection. I love you so much."

I smiled and said, "I love you, too. Now put your cock in my pussy."

Ben penetrated my pussy and I moaned in pleasure. He moved in and out of me slowly using his thumb to rub on my clit to make my pussy get wet. Once my pussy was wet enough, he increased his speed. I said, "I want to stand up."

Ben lifted my body up while his cock was still inside of my pussy. At first, he used his arms to bounce my body up and down. Feeling his strength hold me and control me turned me on. After several minutes, he let me stand and I turned my body around, putting my hands up on the wall. He penetrated me from behind while grabbing my hips for control. I loved the way he pulled my body back and pushed it forward creating such pleasure inside of me.

As I was enjoying Ben moving his cock in and out of my pussy, I felt him put his finger inside of my pussy with his cock. I thought: *This is new*. He moved in and out for a few moments and then moved his hand up from my pussy and slowly inserted his finger, wet with my cum, inside of my asshole. His slow insertion felt warm and sent pleasure through my body. Normally, I was not a big fan of asshole play, but I was enjoying the small tingles he was making at my back door. He hadn't been very experimental with my body in the past and I liked the initiative he was taking. Maybe the inner playboy was finally coming out of him.

Ben continued penetrating my pussy with his cock while pushing his finger that was wet with my cum in and out of my asshole in sync. I was enjoying it. I could feel my pussy and asshole tightening with pleasure. I requested Ben fuck me harder and he did, creating a pleasure inside of me that made my entire body get tight. I embraced the pleasure and when it became too intense, I released an orgasm with a loud moan. Shortly thereafter, I felt Ben cum inside of me.

Ben and I both lay down on the bed to catch our breaths while we enjoyed the pleasure our orgasms created within our bodies. After we caught our breaths, we turned to one another with smiles when Ben said, "I still need to tell you something."

Worried that what he had to say was bad after reading my story, I asked, "Did my story scare you away?"

Ben said, "Quite the opposite. I felt uncomfortable at times, but reading it made me fall more in love with you. Your words were so real, so confusing, but so bittersweet at the same time. My feelings for you were all over the board, however when I finished I realized that I had made the best choice possible in a woman to spend the rest of my life with. I know you mean it when you say you love me. You truly love me and in a way that I never thought someone could fall in love with me."

I was confused as to how my falling in love with Ben was a way in which nobody else could, but it made me feel special and I did love him in a way in which I had never loved another. I said, "I can't believe you read the whole story."

Ben said, "It was hard to put it down. I didn't want to stop reading it and in a strange way, I just wanted to get back to you so we could keep on creating our story."

I said, "Our story is this moment and is perfect in every which way."

Ben said, "I know and that's why I think we should get married now."

I asked, "At this moment? It's almost 10 p.m. How would we get married right now?"

Ben said, "Not tonight, silly."

I asked, "So what does 'right now' mean?"

Ben said, "Let's get married in three weeks. In a month, I am going to have to spend a lot of time in London closing some deals. Let's get married and then go live in my flat in London for a month. While we are there, we can fly to Paris, Rome and anywhere else you want to go."

I asked. "What's your rush?"

Ben said, "I don't know. With you, I am just ready. So many women have come along, but you, well you, Miss Audrey, I just want to be around you all the time."

Feeling smitten, I smiled and asked, "How many women?"

Ben asked, "Do you really want to get into numbers?"

I said, "Actually, no, I don't want to know the number of women you have been with."

Ben said, "Good because I stopped keeping track years ago."

I said, "Damn, you male whore."

Ben asked, "Do you want to tell me your number?"

I said, "I'm not proud of my number, but I'm

not ashamed either if you want to know."

Ben said, "I don't want to know. Marry me. Marry me on the beach somewhere warm. Marry me in a few weeks, Miss Buchanan."

I lay on my side, looking at Ben for a few moments thinking about how this man wanted to marry me. Of all the beautiful women in the world, he picked me. I'd be out of my mind not to accept his crazy invitation to marry him in a few weeks before jet setting to Europe. I loved him wholeheartedly, but as I looked at him, I started to wonder if this fairy tale he was offering me was just a façade like Chase. I mean, what if this man was offering me all these things and love, but actually didn't have it to offer. When I was dating Chase I had no idea he was completely broke and I truly believed he loved me. Maybe my mom always saying that love was blind was true? I always knew Ben was of a different breed, but my recent interaction with Chase had my skepticism running high. I said, "Chase stopped by here last night."

A little shocked, Ben sat up before he asked, "Why?"

I said, "He wanted money. Apparently he's broke and he wants me to advance him the money he is getting for the movie."

Ben asked, "Did you give it to him?"

I said, "No."

Ben asked, "Is Chase always going to be a part of your life?"

I said, "By publishing that memoir I sure asked for it, but I hope not. He only shows up when he needs something and I am hoping that Nikki dragging him out of my place by the ear was enough to keep him out of my life."

Ben asked, "Nikki was here, too?"

I said, "Yes, she walked in when Chase was lying on the ground crying and throwing a temper tantrum."

"How did he get in your house?"

"He put his foot in the door when I slammed it shut on him. I only opened it thinking it was Nikki arriving. Trust me, I didn't want him to come in and once he was in and crying I didn't know how to get rid of him."

Ben asked, "So he wanted your money?"

I said, "Yes, well, he wanted me to prepay him the money he is getting for the movie."

"Audrey, I love you and you can spend as much of our money as you want, but if you are considering helping Chase, I am telling you now that is not an option with me."

I said, "No, I didn't even consider it and I know I have some money, but you have more and I'd never give your money away."

Ben said, "Our money, Audrey. What is mine is yours and I don't want our money going to Chase."

I said, "It won't, but please don't get mad at me for questioning you and your money. It's just that Chase acted like he had all this money and turns out he was broke. Everything just seems too good to be true with you. That scares me and makes me worry it is all a façade too."

Ben said, "Audrey, my money is real. Very real and now it is our money. I'm not bothered by it being spent, but you can't blame me for not wanting it spent on an ex-boyfriend of yours."

"I assure you that your money will never reach the hands of Chase."

"Your money won't either."

I said, "Mine either. He will get his part of the movie deal and that's it."

Ben said, "In my opinion, he doesn't even deserve that, but I respect your decision to include him in the deal."

I said, "I wouldn't have had a story if I never met him so it was only fair he got a portion."

Ben said, "About your writing..."

With hesitation I said, "Yes, about my writing?"

"When I came in tonight the first thing I wanted to say to you was that I feel honored and loved that you included me as a part of one of your stories."

I asked, "Really? I can't believe my sexual mishaps didn't scare you away."

"No, reading your story actually made me fall in love with you more."

"How? I mean, I did some crazy shit while we were talking."

"I know and it made me a little

uncomfortable, but the realness of what happened combined with it leading you to fall in love with me was beautiful."

"I just get mad at myself because you were in my reach and I was off doing nonsense."

Ben said, "Audrey, I've been in that position. I've done stupid stuff. Tons of stupid stuff, but I only did those things because I was in a phase, a growing phase, where I wasn't aware of what could be."

I gave Ben a light kiss on the lips and said, "I'm so glad you are back in Chicago with me!"

Ben said, "Me too," before pulling me in and spooning me.

We lay quietly in the buff for a few moments before I pulled the blanket over us for warmth. I felt Ben squeeze my body tighter, knowing I was cold. I asked, "So, you really want to get married in three weeks?"

Ben said, "That's funny you said that because I was just thinking the same thing."

I said, "Oh really?"

Ben said, "I say, let's get married in three weeks."

I asked, "Really, three weeks as in twenty-one days?"

Ben said, "See, you aren't that bad at math. Yes, twenty-one days."

"What is your hurry?"

"I'm just really excited to be married to you because you are the first girl I have met that I've wanted to marry."

I said, "Ben, can I ask you something?"

Ben said, "Yes, darling."

I asked, "Are you the type of person that buys the crap in the check out aisles or the end of aisle displays?"

Ben said, "No, not really. Sometimes I grab some chocolate, but my maid Ula in New York did most of my grocery shopping."

I said, "It's just that this has all moved really fast and I worry that after we rush into all this, you might regret your quick impulse purchase."

"What are you talking about? I've thought about this moment for years. This is exactly how I imagined it. I lived a very great New York lifestyle and had nice things, but you've seen my place and I didn't have anything elaborate. Literally, my life for the past nine years consisted of me working most of the time and, on occasion, humoring women to satisfy my sexual needs. I saved and invested and invested more until the day came where I had met my financial goal."

"How much money do you actually have? I mean, owning and operating a private jet has to cost a pretty penny and you wrote a check for one and a half million dollars like it was nothing when we bought the old warehouse."

Ben said, "This stays between us."

I said, "Of course."

Ben said, "I have forty-two million

dollars that the U.S. Government knows about."

I yelled out, "What!" and when I yelled, a fart snuck out of my ass and blew on Ben's naked balls.

Ben said, "You just farted on my balls!"

I started laughing and said, "I'm sorry," as I turned over. I continued by asking, "Did you say you have forty-two million dollars that the U.S. Government knows about?"

Ben said, "Yes, and that kind of takes me to why I'd like to get married in three weeks."

I asked, "What, are you doing something illegal and you are going to end up in jail so you need to marry me to hold on to your money?"

Ben laughed, "No, but that would make for a good story for you."

I said, "Fuck yeah, that would. I might use that for my next book. I like that idea."

Ben said, "In about a month, I have to go to London for six weeks to finish up some really big deals. That's why I want us to go there as an extended honeymoon."

I said, "We don't have to be married for me to go to London with you."

"I just thought it would be nice. We could go for a week on an exotic honeymoon and then head to London. While in London, we can jet set all over Europe."

I said, "Pinch me, Ben."

Ben asked, "What?"

I put my arm in front of Ben and said, "Pinch me. Just do it."

Ben said, "I'm not going to pinch you. Instead, I will kiss you."

Ben gave me a long passionate kiss and I felt myself smiling the whole time. After we pulled away from our kiss I said, "Is this all real? I mean, seriously, I've never read a book or seen a movie that was this good."

Ben laughed a little before he said, "Yes, this is all real. Do you want to travel to Europe with me?"

I said, "Umm, yeah! My PR agent, Steven, is not going to be happy about this."

Ben said, "Your publisher and book agent will love it because you are going to have plenty of time to write."

"I've always dreamt of sitting in little cafes in Europe writing so you have no idea how much this means to me!"

Ben hesitated as he asked, "So, yes?"

I said, "Yes! Yes! Yes!" before kissing Ben and slowly moving my body on top of his. I could feel his cock getting hard underneath me as we kissed. I stopped for a moment and placed both my hands on his face as I said, "I love you so much, Ben!"

Ben said, "I love you more, my darling."

After Ben told me he loved me, I went back to kissing him. Once his cock was hard, he slipped it inside of my pussy. I moved my body up and down as his cock disappeared inside of my pussy. He leaned back and watched me. I slowly moved up and down, enjoying each moment and feeling my pussy get more and more wet. I was enjoying the slow tender fuck, but then Ben put his hands on my hips leading me to go faster. I didn't want to go faster, but I wanted to make him feel as good as he had been making me feel so I followed his lead.

I could feel my pussy tightening up very slowly, but I wasn't pleasured as fast as Ben had been because a few moments later I felt his cock pulsate inside of my pussy and he came. I was a little disappointed and surprised he was able to cum so fast because we had just had sex, but I was glad he was feeling good.

We lay down cuddling and moments later I felt Ben fall asleep holding me. I looked out the window thinking about what had just happened. I felt so happy inside, but kept wondering what the catch was. This was all too good to be true. How could a man walk into my life and everything change in an instant?

The next morning I woke up to Ben yelling in the living room. I had never heard him raise his voice in such a way. I lay there for a few moments, listening to his words and realizing he was upset about some investment. I went to bed thinking that I had this perfect man, but maybe I had found his imperfection. I didn't like the feeling that was building up inside of me by listening to him yell. It was a big turn off. He was always so kind and gentle around me. I decided I should hop out of bed to peek my head out the door thinking that Ben seeing me might get him to stop yelling at the person at the other end of the line.

When I sat up, my head felt a little light so I shook my head and felt okay, but when I stood up my entire body felt weak. From there I blacked out and woke up with Ben standing above me. His face was full of concern and he kissed my forehead the moment I opened my eyes. I asked, "What happened?"

Ben said, "I was in the living room and I heard a crash. I came running in the room and you had passed out."

I asked, "Did I hit my face? My right cheek

hurts."

Ben said, "I think so. I'll go grab some ice. Stay put for a moment."

I stared up at the ceiling while I listened to Ben run and get some ice in the kitchen. When he came back in the room, he put the ice on my cheek and I raised my hand up to hold it in place. He then lifted my body up and put me on the bed. I said, "I remember feeling lightheaded when I sat up and then I don't remember anything after that."

Ben said, "Did you eat dinner before I got home last night?"

I said, "No, I haven't had much of an appetite."

Ben said, "Lie here. I ran to the store because I was going to make you breakfast in bed, but then I got caught on the phone."

I asked, "Who were you yelling at?"

Ben said, "Oh, I'm sorry you had to hear that. One of my business partners was supposed to have finished a few things yesterday and did not. It might cost us a pretty penny. You won't hear me yell like that again."

I asked, "Do you yell like that often?"

Ben said, "I am very serious when it comes to business."

I said, "I didn't like hearing that."

"I'll do my best to keep my business separate from you. When we have our new place, my office will be a whole floor down from the bedroom so you won't hear a peep from me."

"Ben, you shouldn't yell like that though. I'm sure your business partner didn't screw up on purpose."

"My business is my business. Anywhere else in life you can boss me around, but I ask that you not interfere with my work."

I had found Ben's flaw. I went to bed the night before thinking he was perfect, but woke up realizing that he had a controlling nature about him when it came to business. I think all along I could sense that, but tried to ignore it. I simply said, "Okay, your business is your business."

Ben said, "Thank you. Now relax here and I'll go make you some breakfast," before he kissed my forehead and walked out to the kitchen.

When Ben came back with my breakfast, I ate it feeling myself pulling away from Ben. I was quiet as I slowly ate my scrambled eggs. Ben looked at me with a look like he knew something was wrong. He said, "Audrey, I'm really sorry you heard me yell, but it was a situation that warranted me raising my voice."

I said, "I know, I know. I don't know why it is bothering me. Maybe it is because I feel so tired, causing me to feel anxious. Can we talk about something pleasant?"

Ben said, "Of course. How about we talk about our wedding?"

I said, "Ben, we don't need to get married in

order for me to go to Europe with you. We can go and have a pre-honeymoon and then get married next spring somewhere warm."

Ben asked, "Why wait though?"

I had no reason to rush into getting married, but I had no reason to wait either. I knew I was feeling skeptical about Ben's yelling, but I loved him and I wanted to marry him. Ben went on to tell me he could hire a wedding planner to plan everything and that my only worry would be finding myself the perfect dress. My mother would love to plan my wedding, but I knew my mother wouldn't want to plan a destination wedding. I figured she could have a reception for us over the summer when we were back from Europe. She'd love to have a "hoe down" for us with our family and friends at our lake house. Not having to plan a wedding was exactly what I wanted and Ben was handing it to me on a silver platter. I said, "Okay, let's do it. Let's get married and then go to Europe!"

Ben said, "Great! Make an invite list and I'll do the rest."

I asked, "Can't we just do a Facebook invite?"

Ben said, "I think it should just be family and close friends."

I said, "Alright. Give me a day and I'll have a list. I'm going to have to call my mom."

Ben said, "Future Mrs. Wright, you are my Mrs. Wright!"

I said, "Hey, I call you Mr. Wright!"

Ben laughed when he said, "We are just so 'Wright' for one another."

That afternoon I called my mom to tell her the news. She was ecstatic, to say the least. She had so many ideas for a reception at the lake house, but kept asking what she could do to plan the wedding in the Caribbean. I told her the wedding planner would take care of it all, but I needed her to send me a list of the family members she thought should be invited. She started rattling names and I had to stop her. I told her I just wanted it to be aunts, uncles and cousins, when I realized that my immediate family consisted of almost eighty people. Shit. I put my phone on mute and said to Ben, "My family is like eighty people."

Ben laughed and said, "That's fine."

I said, "I'm sure most of them won't want to pay to go to the Caribbean so it should be okay."

Ben said, "No, they won't be paying. We'll cover the trip for everyone."

I said, "No, Ben if we, actually, if you pay for them to attend the wedding, they will all show up!"

Ben said, "That's great. I can't wait to meet them all."

I continued the conversation with my mom, telling her we'd be sending out an email with all of the information in the next couple of days. I asked if she could send me email addresses for all the family members. She said she would put together a list and start calling everyone as soon as we got off the phone. I held on and prolonged my conversation for a few more minutes knowing that it would be much harder to turn back once I got off the phone and my mom started calling family members. When my mother said to me, "Audrey, you've found your prince and I couldn't be happier to know that my daughter is going to live a fairy tale." I knew I shouldn't prolong our conversation any longer. My mother was right and I was embarking on a journey of a lifetime with an amazing man. Sure, everything was moving fast, but I was truly enjoying each moment. What girl wouldn't? I had found what every single girl was out there looking for.

After I got off the phone with my mom, I walked out of my bedroom and said to Ben, "Let's get married in Punta Cana."

Ben said, "Done."

I said, "Awesome. Want to go to dinner with Nikki and Bree tonight?"

Ben said, "Sounds great. Where do you want to go? I'll make reservations."

I said, "Let's go to Tanta."

Ben called and made reservations for 8 p.m. Once he got off the phone I sent a group text to Bree and Nikki asking them to meet us. Bree responded to the group message asking if Scotty could come and I told her yes and then Nikki said she was going to be bringing her latest fling that she had met on Tinder. Ben asked if I was going to ask them to be bridesmaids and I told him I wasn't planning on it. He then asked who I wanted to stand up in our wedding and I said we didn't need a bridal party. Ben really wanted his niece Carly to have a part in the wedding and his brother-in-law Bo to be his best man. I thought about it for a moment and said I couldn't pick between Nikki and Bree to have as a maid of honor. After a couple minutes of conversing, Ben convinced me that Bree and Nikki could both be my maids of honor, he'd have Bo be his best man and Carly would be our flower girl. I told Ben no more people in the wedding party. I wanted things simple and he agreed that was it.

We met Bree and Nikki for dinner and they were ecstatic about the news of our wedding date being just around the corner. When they found out Ben was covering all costs of travel and that they'd get to ride on our private jet, their jaws dropped. I still had no idea where we were getting married in Punta Cana, but, knowing what Ben had come up with for us over the past few months, I knew it would be good. Bree said we needed to start looking for a wedding dress as soon as possible so I told her we could go Saturday. Excited about her duties as half maid of honor, she said she'd schedule the appointments. I was lucky to have a responsible friend like Bree and a fiancé who loved taking care of shit like appointments and planning.

Saturday morning Ben woke me up bright and early. I felt very tired so I begged for an extra five minutes of sleep. Ben gave me five more minutes three times before he said I had to get going so I wouldn't be late. Once I was showered and dressed, Bree called saying she and Nikki were downstairs waiting for me. I figured they had a cab, but when I got downstairs there was a limo waiting for me. I got inside and Nikki explained Ben had gotten us a limo for the day. Bree popped open the bottle of champagne and poured us each a glass before we toasted to my future with Ben.

As we drove to the first boutique, Bree requested wedding logistics from me. I told her that Ben wanted us to have our wedding at one of his business partner's houses in Punta Cana, but there wasn't enough room there for my big family so the wedding planner had us all booked at the Hard Rock Hotel in Punta Cana. I was actually happy about this because it gave us all a little space from one another, but we could still have a good time.

We arrived at the first boutique and the staff was ready for us. I was starting to get used to this kind of VIP treatment, but in a small way, I actually missed being the little guy. There was far less pressure when nobody cared. I enjoyed it though because Ben calling ahead and flashing his money gave me champagne while I shopped. We literally sat on a couch while the women in the store brought dress after dress out for us to look at. I said "No" a couple dozen times before a woman brought out a chiffon dress with a sweetheart neck. I said, "That's the one."

Nikki said, "It's so plain, Audrey."

I stood up and asked the woman to hand it to me before walking into the dressing room. Bree walked in behind me to help me zip up. As she was zipping me up I said, "This is the dress."

Bree said, "We have two more boutiques to go to."

I said, "No need. This is the dress."

I walked out of the dressing room and did a twirl. Nikki said, "It's plain, but it is so you, Audrey. You are right; this is the dress for you."

I looked in the mirror at myself and I smiled. Every fantasy I had about falling in love was being lived out by the moment. The perfect man, the perfect dress, the perfect location, a man my family approved of, the traveling, and the love. My smile slowly went down and Nikki asked, "What's wrong?"

I said, "Nothing."

Nikki said, "Audrey, what's wrong?"

I asked, "Is Ben my great love?"

Nikki said, "Of course he is and you know I wouldn't just say that. He's the one and the moment you stop questioning that will be the moment you will feel true happiness."

I said, "I've read hundreds of books and if they've taught me anything it's that a love isn't a great love unless it's tragic."

"Audrey, your life isn't a book. Your life is real. Yes, your life with Chase was a great book, but that's only because you were living in a fantasy. Your life with him wasn't real. This, Ben, your wedding, well these are all real and they are all good. Embrace it. Enjoy it. Be fucking grateful for it, bitch! I've been searching for a man to love me like Ben loves you for years."

I said, "I have been hoping for it, too."

Nikki said, "Then quit fucking questioning it! You look amazing in this dress and you are going to look beautiful on your wedding day. Ben loves you, I mean he's a fucking millionaire and he could have any girl he wants, but he is head over heels in love with you."

I said, "I know you are right and I am going to let go of the doubt inside of me. I'm about to get married! I should be happy and enjoying each and every moment!"

Nikki said, "Good, now put some fucking weight on before the wedding because you are too fucking skinny."

The woman who brought me the dress said, "No, don't put on weight. We don't have much time to get this dress perfectly fit to your body."

I said, "I'll try not to."

Nikki, Bree and I finished the bottle of champagne at the bridal boutique and then headed out the door. Bree asked what we should do next since I had found a dress and didn't need to go to our appointments at the other boutiques. Nikki said, "Let's go to dive bars and get shitfaced."

I said, "I don't know. Ben's home alone today and I feel like I'm abandoning him."

Nikki said, "He's becoming a Chicago resident so he's going to need to learn how to be on his own. You can't be by his side all the time."

I said, "True, but he hasn't had the time to make friends here yet."

Nikki said, "He thinks you are going to be looking for a wedding dress all day so I'm sure he made plans or he is home getting a boner doing work."

Bree asked, "Did you just say he is getting a boner doing work?"

Nikki said, "Ben's idea of talking dirty is talking about money."

Bree asked, "Really?"

I said, "Yeah, he gets turned on by talking about me spending his money."

Bree said, "He must have a controlling personality."

I said, "Only when it comes to work."

Bree said, "Be careful with that. Psychologically speaking and from my experience that could lead into control issues."

I said, "Don't get me started. I've been struggling with that all week, but I don't want to think about that right now. I think Nikki's idea to bar hop and get drunk midday is a great idea. Where should we start?"

Nikki said, "Let's start in Wrigleyville and then go to River North. Wrigleyville is always filled with young men in the afternoons."

The neighborhood of Chicago called Wrigleyville was always full of young men day drinking so I said, "Mr. Limo Driver, take us to Wrigleyville!"

We went to Wrigleyville and our first stop was at a restaurant and bar called Moe's. When we got there I began to feel tired, but I fought it. My age really must've been getting to me. I drank some Red Bull and started feeling on par again. There was a group of young, fresh out of college boys at the bar we were at on a bar crawl. They hit on us and that stroked our egos, but we didn't stay long. We left there to have a drink at Deuces and then got in the limo to head to River North hoping we'd find men our age. When the driver got to River North, we directed him to take us to El Hefe, hoping there would be a fun afternoon party happening. I started feeling tipsy so I decided to text Ben and tell him what I was up to. He said he was at the Trump, meeting with a possible investing partner and he was glad I was having a good time. I told him I was, but I was ready to go home. He said since he was just down the street he could pick me up after his meeting. I responded telling him that I would love for him to pick me up.

I had a margarita and tried enjoying

myself, but when Ben texted me and said he was leaving the Trump, I decided to pull a Houdini and sneak outside to leave. I knew drunk Nikki and Bree wouldn't let me leave if I told them I wanted to go home. When I got outside, I saw Ben get out of a cab to pick me up. I ran up to him and in my drunken run I'm sure I looked like a fool, but I was so glad to see him and go home. I got into the cab and on our drive home I snuggled into Ben the whole time. Ben asked, "Did you miss me?"

I said, "Terribly. Thank you for saving me from my wild girlfriends."

Ben said, "Anytime. Did you find a wedding dress?"

I said, "Yes, the perfect dress. It looks like the one I've always envisioned. I hope you like it."

Ben said, "I'm sure I'll love it. I sent the travel information to all of your relatives today. I hope they can all make it."

I said, "If it's a free trip, you can expect that they will all be there."

Ben said, "Good. I can't wait to meet them all. Your parents, grandmother and friends will travel with us on the jet and the wedding planner will book the rest of your family on a flight to arrive later that day."

I asked, "How did I get so lucky to find a planner like you?"

Ben said, "Opposites attract. You've actually had me creatively thinking about new investment ideas."

I asked, "Really?"

"Yes, I was just in a meeting discussing new investments in film."

I jokingly said, "I have a movie coming out. Do you want to invest in that?"

Ben laughed and said, "You are getting a nice chunk of change for that. Let's keep our businesses separate."

I said, "Good idea."

Ben asked, "How drunk are you?"

I said, "Drunk, really drunk."

"You are quite the happy drunk."

I said, "What's not to be happy about? I am about to marry the most wonderful man in the world with the most beautiful dress."

Ben said, "That's what I like to hear."

A week before our wedding Ben had to leave to go to New York for a couple of days and I was busy wrapping up book stuff with my agent and Steven. After a couple of weeks of deliberation, I decided to publish my memoir *Time for Me*, which was the follow up story to my memoir *Dating Chase Walker*. We decided the title *Time for Audrey Buchanan* was more fitting though. The support of Ben, my mother, Nikki, and my agent made the decision easy. The book was going to go through editing while I was gone for my wedding in Punta Cana and honeymoon in Bali and Europe. Things were working out perfectly, almost too perfectly, but I wasn't about to start questioning it. Nikki was right and I just needed to enjoy each moment.

My aunts and cousins put together a shower/bachelorette party for me the Saturday before we were to leave for Punta Cana. Ben had to leave town for a bachelor party in Las Vegas his brother-in-law had planned and then he was going to California for a few days so I wouldn't see him until our flight to Punta Cana. I was anxious about spending so much time away from Ben, but knew that distance could only do us good.

I woke up before Ben the morning of his flight by crawling under the covers and sucking on his cock. We had become an old couple and hadn't been indulging in oral sex as much. When I was under the covers sucking on his flaccid cock, I heard him moan while he stretched his body. Soon his flaccid cock became hard in my mouth and I was turned on feeling it become harder and harder. I slowly moved my mouth up and down and once it was hard, I crawled up from under the sheets and starting kissing Ben's mouth after apologizing for my morning breath. Ben laughed as he joked that he liked my morning breath.

After kissing Ben, I grabbed his hard cock with my right hand and led it into my pussy. As I inserted it into my pussy, I let out a moan feeling it push inside of me. I moved up and down at a slow pace allowing my pussy to get wet. Once wet, I began to move faster. As I moved faster, Ben placed his finger on my clit, moving it in a circular motion and creating extra sensation to run through my body. Feeling pleasure run through my body, I grabbed my boobs wanting to squeeze my nipples to create more sensation to run through my body. As I grabbed my boobs and began squeezing them in pleasure, I felt something that didn't seem right in my right boob causing me to stop for a moment and unknowingly make a strange face. Ben asked, "Did you just cum? If so, that was the strangest 'O' face I have ever seen."

I said, "No, give me your hand. I think there's a lump in my boob."

I led Ben's hand up to touch my boob and he said, "That does feel weird."

I said, "I've never felt that before."

He asked, "Could it be a part of your implant?"

I said, "Maybe. I don't know. I guess I haven't been touching my tits lately. Does it feel strange to you?"

Ben said, "I love your boobs, they are beautiful, but I'm a butt guy so I pay much more attention to that."

I said, "It's probably nothing. I'm sorry for disturbing our sex session."

Ben said, "Go the doctor before we leave for our trip so we won't have to worry."

I said, "It's probably nothing. Breast implants feel strange and with all the weight I've lost lately my body feels different. I'm sure it's nothing. Let's get back to fucking."

Ben said, "I'm sorry, but I've kind of lost my hard on."

I said, "No, I'll suck your cock again and get it hard."

"Oh, darling, you are so sweet, but I should get in the shower and head out the door. Will you promise me that you will go to the doctor before we leave for Punta Cana?"

I said, "Yeah, but I'm sure it's nothing."

Ben said, "I'm sure it's nothing too, but if we get the all clear from the doctor, we won't be worried during our wedding or while we are globetrotting."

I said, "I can't believe I am going to spend six weeks in Europe!"

Ben left and I went back to sleep for a few hours before my parents arrived. My mother wanted to join me for my last wedding dress fitting so they were taking me to the boutique and then driving me home with them for a bridal shower at my aunt's house. My mother sent me text updates on how far they were from my place and when she said they were turning onto my street I put my coat on, grabbed my overnight bag and went downstairs. My mother jumped out of the car and ran toward me all excited when she saw me. I laughed as she hugged me and asked, "Mom, why are you so excited?"

My mom responded, "Because my baby is getting married in less than a week!"

I giggled at my mom and crawled into the back seat of my dad's car. He looked back and smiled at me before he said, "Love looks good on you, kiddo."

I smiled back at my dad and said, "Thanks, Dad."

I acted like a backseat driver trying to navigate our way to the bridal boutique. When we arrived a girl welcomed me by name and then asked us to follow her to the back. My mother whispered, "This place is so fancy. I'm surprised your dress didn't cost more money."

I said, "I honestly think I bought the cheapest dress in the whole store."

My mom said, "Like I always told you; it's not the price of clothing, it is how clothing makes you feel."

My parents sat down on a couch before a woman walked behind the curtain to assist me into my dress. After the woman zipped me up, I stood and looked at myself in the mirror for a few moments. I thought to myself how the dress was perfect in every way and then I started thinking about how I couldn't believe I was about to get married. I smiled at myself in the mirror and excitedly did a mini twirl of a dance behind the curtain before I walked out to show my parents the dress.

When I walked out wearing the wedding dress in front of my parents for the first time, I felt a little emotional. My mother had tears in her eyes and my father looked at me like I was still his little girl. In seeing their emotion, I could feel their happiness. My mother said, "It is just perfect, Audrey. You look stunning."

I smiled at my mom and then my dad said, "It's gorgeous, kiddo. You look so grown up."

My mom said, "She does look so grown up. Oh, our little baby girl is getting married."

I asked, "So you like the dress? I mean, you kind of have to because it's too late to get another one."

My mom said, "Audrey, I love it. You are going to make the most beautiful bride, but after the wedding you need to put some weight on. I can see your bones. I know you lost weight after you and Chase broke up, but you look too skinny."

My dad said, "Don't bring up Chase. Audrey has always been slim. I'm sure she and Ben will be eating at all sorts of amazing restaurants in Europe and she will come back with some meat on her bones."

My mom said, "I hope so. She needs a healthy body to give me a grandchild."

I said, "Oh my God, Mom, grandchildren are a long way off."

My mom said, "You never know. Look how fast things happened with Ben. I bet a few months ago you never thought you'd be getting married so fast."

I said, "That's true, but I am not ready to have a baby. I don't even know if I am going to make a good wife. I mean, I rarely clean up after myself."

My mom said, "Things will change when you get married. You'll be cooking and cleaning and enjoying it."

I said, "Eww, no."

My dad said, "It's a good thing Ben can afford to get you a cleaning lady and probably a personal chef, too."

We left the bridal boutique and my father

strategically placed my wedding gown in the back of his SUV. I sent a text to Ben just to tell him I loved him and that I had the perfect dress. He responded with a smiley emojicon. After texting Ben and navigating my father to the highway, I closed my eyes and dozed off for the rest of the car ride. I needed some rest before spending time with my loud aunts and cousins at my bridal shower.

We arrived at my aunt's house and it was strange that I was the center of attention. Usually, at family parties I would be an observer. I did notice I got a little more attention over the holidays because of my fifteen minutes of fame from my memoir being published, but that attention was nothing compared to the excitement everyone had over me getting married. I liked all the excitement, but as with any family, people still have to throw out a few zingers. My Aunt Margie said to me she never thought she'd see the day I'd get married and my Aunt Irene said she hoped I wouldn't blow it with Ben before he said 'I do' in a few days. Their little zingers actually made me feel more comfortable with the whole situation.

When my grandmother walked over by me with her cane in one hand and a can of Pabst Blue Ribbon in the other, I knew she had something on her mind to tell me. She ousted my two cousins off the couch and sat down next to me. I said, "Hi Grandma."

My grandma smiled at me and said, "Audrey, this is your story here."

I said, "I know, Grams, and I am trying to enjoy every moment of it."

My grandma looked at me and said, "You are not understanding what I am saying. This right here is your story. I liked Chase, but only because he whispered things in my ear that made me feel pretty. Things a young man shouldn't say to a woman my age, but nonetheless, what he said made me feel beautiful and I miss that with your grandfather being gone. Chase was just creative material to you and you were just another one of the women that will come into his life to help him settle his insecurities."

I said, "Grandma, what?"

My grandma said, "No, keep listening to me, Audrey. I'm old so that makes me wise."

I said, "Okay, I'm listening."

My grandmother took a sip of her Pabst Blue Ribbon before continuing. "Don't stop writing your story yet. Even if you never want to share it with anyone, keep on writing. Chase Walker isn't your story. In fact, your story is being written right now and I want to tell you that I am okay with you talking about me in your stories."

I said, "Noted, Grandma."

"Your love with Chase wasn't real and that's why it made a good story, but your love with Ben is real and that's why it is going to make a great story."

"Don't you think people would get bored reading a story where everything is fucking amazing and happy?"

My grandma said, "Would you rather live a story where there's a bunch of nonsense happening with a crazy man or would you rather live a story where love is real and life is grand?"

I said, "I'll take the latter."

My grandma said, "Exactly. Don't end your story where Chase walked away from you."

I said, "I actually didn't. I continued the story and I think I am going to publish it. It is being edited as we speak."

My grandma said, "Good, I'm glad you continued writing your story."

I said, "I appreciate your advice and I'll be sure to include this conversation in my story."

"Good. Now, I can't believe I am flying on a private jet for your wedding. I haven't been on an airplane since 1984."

I asked, "Grandma, do you have a passport?"

My grandma said, "Yeah, I had to rush it and it cost me over eighty dollars. This is the first time I am leaving this country. I'm glad you are giving me a free lift on your private jet. My friend Eunice paid over four-hundred dollars to fly to see her grandkids in Texas."

I said, "Grams, it means the world to me that you are going to be at my wedding."

My grandma said, "I wouldn't miss it my dear unless there's no PBR on your private jet or at the resort. If there's no PBR, I'm staying home."

I said, "I promise there will be plenty of cans of PBR for you. Ben is making sure."

My grandma said, "I knew I liked him for a reason."

I left my bridal shower that night thinking about what my grandmother had said and realized she was right. There was so much left of my story to tell and as fucked up as my relationship was with Chase, he was the one who screwed with my head enough to start getting me writing in the right direction. So, as much as the man creeped me out for believing he was the messenger of God, I had a soft spot in my heart for him for inspiring me.

I woke up Wednesday morning and I stared up at the ceiling fan going around and around. I thought about how I was about to get on an airplane, an airplane I owned, and head off to the Caribbean to get married. I, Audrey Buchanan, who was very single at this time last year, was about to get married to the sweetest man who had ever loved me. I felt tired and didn't want to get out of bed, but I had to because I so badly wanted to marry Ben with every beat of my heart.

I slowly dragged myself out of bed and when I got into my bathroom, I looked in the mirror. Even though I had almost nine hours of sleep, my face looked tired and my body, well my body was too skinny. I never meant to look so skinny, but my life had changed so much over the past few months that I thought it must have been taking a toll on my weight. As I stared at my naked body, I vowed to get my weight up after the wedding. I continued staring at myself in the mirror when I lifted my right arm and felt my breast for the lump I had found. I told Ben I would visit a doctor to get it checked out; however, I never made it to any doctor. With my left hand, I moved my fingers around feeling for the lump, but I could barely feel it so I was sure it was nothing. I looked into the mirror for a few more moments and said, "After the wedding, when I am traveling the world, I am going to make my health my first priority."

After my little pep talk, I got into the shower before getting dressed and ready to leave the country for the next seven weeks. I had three large suitcases ready at the door when the limo driver called to say he was out front. I told him I was about ready and he said he would be upstairs in a few minutes to take my luggage. I did a final scan of my bedroom and bathroom to make sure I had everything I needed and then I did some final unplugging of appliances throughout my apartment. When the driver knocked on my door, I felt anxiousness grow in my body. I realized that I was about to leave on a trip that would change my life forever.

The driver took two of my suitcases down and when he came back up for the third one, I followed him out the door after turning off the lights and locking the door behind me. As I was locking the door, I realized that when we got back to Chicago our new home would be ready and I wouldn't be calling this place mine for much longer. My life was changing faster than I could ever imagine and I was living a fairy tale.

I got into the limo and when I did I saw a

bouquet of my favorite kind of flowers, white daisies. I smiled, knowing Ben had sent them. Once I sat inside the limo, I noticed a box of donuts from Glazed and Infused. When I opened the box, all the donuts were shaped like engagement rings. A smile spread across my face. When I spotted the bottle of champagne sitting on ice, well, I knew exactly why I had fallen in love with Ben in the first place. The limo picked up Nikki next and then Bree. Once we were all in the limo, we popped open the bottle of champagne with a cheer. Nikki's latest man and Scotty Stylez sat at one end of the limo talking to each other while Nikki, Bree and I excitedly celebrated what was about to come.

The limo drove us right up to the jet at O'Hare Airport and when we got out I spotted my father standing on the stairs to the jet, excitedly waving to us. He yelled out, "I got your dress on the plane safe and sound, kiddo! Don't worry, I made sure Ben didn't see it!"

I laughed at my father's remark as I walked up the stairs into the airplane. When I got on the plane, I saw Ben and for some reason I started crying. Ben walked up to me and asked, "Why are you crying?"

I said, "I have no idea. I guess I am just that fucking happy."

Ben smiled at me before kissing me on the forehead. After he kissed me he said, "I would never want to make you cry, but if I ever made you cry, I'd hope that it would be from pure happiness."

I said, "Ben, I still feel like you need to pinch me."

Ben smiled and then gave me a slight pinch on the butt before he said, "This is no dream, Audrey. This is our flight to our future."

I smiled at Ben and then grabbed his hand. I wanted to hold his hand starting now and forever because he could lead me into so much happiness and protect me from pain. Ben smiled at me and then gave me one more kiss on the forehead before leading us down the aisle of the airplane. As we walked, I saw my grandmother look at me and give me a smile. It was a smile that was just for me, which made me feel happy inside. My grandmother was a big joker and quite an asshole, but her words at my bridal shower and this smile let me know that I was exactly where I was supposed to be, that this moment was just one of many blissful moments to come.

Everybody took a seat on the plane and then an attendant came out with a tray full of poured champagne. We each took a glass and before the flight took off Ben stood up and spoke on both of our behalves. He told the plane full of our closest family and friends how he was excited for the days ahead where we'd all get to know each other and become a family. I couldn't believe I was going to be related to Bo Brady. The hottest guy in Hollywood was on an airplane my fiancé and I owned and he was about to become my brother-in-law. Talk about zero to sixty.

During the flight I heard conversations of excursions people wanted to go on and things people wanted to do at the resort. Their ideas seemed like good ones, but in all honesty at that very moment all I wanted to do was to take a nap. I wanted to be excited about all that was happening, but my body was still feeling exhausted. Ben looked at me and then put his arm around my shoulder before he said, "Snuggle into me and let's take a little nap while everyone is distracted. Once we land, all eyes will be on us wondering what to do and where to go."

I didn't say anything to Ben. I just snuggled into him and closed my eyes. While my eyes were closed, Ben whispered in my ear asking how my doctor's visit went. I just mumbled, "Fine" and then dozed off in his arms.

I slept for a good hour before I woke up to my mom poking me. She said, "Audrey, you can't sleep the whole flight. Everyone is excited so come join the conversation."

I rubbed my eyes a little and then unbuckled my seatbelt to go talk to everyone. Ben had already somehow shifted my head to rest on the window and he was up playing cards with the guys near the front of the plane. I walked up to say hi to Ben first and when he saw me he smiled as he told me he was winning. I said, "Good" before kissing him and looking to find the flight attendant to get me some champagne. While I stood waiting for the flight attendant to pour my champagne, I was next to the bathroom. I wondered how Ben and I could sneak in there to fuck. That would for sure wake me up. I needed a pick-me-up like a quickie to get me moving, but there was no way someone wouldn't notice we were both gone. Plus, the door was visible to everyone. I'd have to wait until we got to the resort for a quick fuck pick-me-up and save our next airplane fuck for our flight to Bali from Punta Cana.

I took my champagne and sat down next to Nikki and Bree. They told me I needed to start drinking faster to catch up with them. They were a few drinks ahead of me and full of giggles. I asked, "What's with all the giggles?"

In her goofy drunken whisper voice, Bree said, "We are on our friend's private jet with Bo Brady."

Nikki said in a whisper, "Yeah, Bo fucking Brady!"

I laughed and said, "I felt a similar way the first time I met him."

Nikki whispered, "His wife is a little bitchy though. No wonder we never see her in the tabloids."

I put my pointer finger up to my mouth, motioning Nikki to be quiet. I whispered, "I'm still trying to get his sister, Catherine, to like me so be extra nice to her."

Nikki said, "But she's so snobby."

Bree cut in and said, "We got this, Audrey. Catherine will love you before you say 'I do.'"

I talked with Nikki and Bree a little longer before getting up to get another glass of champagne and sitting down next to my mother, grandmother and Ben's mother, Sherry. When I sat down my mother said, "Audrey, I was just telling your grandmother and Sherry my surprise for you for your wedding."

I questioned, "Oh, a surprise?"

My mother said, "Yes, and I am so excited that I can't wait until we get to Punta Cana to tell you."

I asked, "What's the surprise? Tell me!"

My mother said, "I know you and Ben have a grand suite you are staying in, but your father booked a suite for Friday night just for you and me. We are going to have a sleepover!"

Ben's mother said, "I think it's such a nice idea. You don't want to see Ben before the wedding because it's bad luck."

I was thinking to myself how we were living in the twenty-first century, but my mom seemed so excited about our sleepover and I wanted to keep kissing up to Ben's mom so I said, "We should have a bachelorette party in our girl's suite that night."

My mother said, "What a lovely idea!"

My grandmother said, "I'll only be there if there's PBR. Like I told you, if this resort doesn't have my beer, I am leaving."

I said, "Grandma, Ben already made sure that you will have plenty of PBR the whole time we are there. Don't you worry."

My grandma said, "Alright, I just worry that these foreigners won't carry American beer."

When we arrived in Punta Cana, everyone was focused on customs and taking everything in. When we arrived at the resort, we each checked into our rooms. Ben and I got into our suite and I crashed down on the bed. Ben laughed at me, but I said, "Get naked."

Ben jokingly questioned, "Now? Before our wedding?"

I said, "Yes, right now. Get naked and come over here so I can put your cock in my mouth."

Ben smiled and took his clothes off quickly before getting on top of me and putting his cock in my mouth. His legs were straddled over my chest while I moved his cock in and out of my mouth. I used my left hand to rub his shaft while my right hand gently massaged his balls. I looked at him with a little smile while his cock was in my mouth and Ben said, "There is nothing hotter than seeing you smile with my cock in your mouth."

I continued smiling and making eye contact with Ben while I pleasured him. After several minutes Ben stopped me and said, "I want to fuck you before I cum."

He moved off of me and then began assisting me as I took my clothing off. Once naked, Ben said, "Let me fuck you right now."

Ben and I hadn't had much foreplay in the past few weeks so I stood up on the bed and in a demanding voice said, "You can't fuck me until you eat my pussy!"

Ben gave me a sexy smile and then put his mouth on my pussy. I moaned in pleasure. It had been too long since he licked my clit and warmed me up. I was not about to allow us to become an old married couple who went straight to penetration when it came to sex. I took my hands and grabbed my boobs, but quickly took my right hand off when I felt the lump again. I didn't need that kind of turn off. I kept my left hand on my left breast and put my right hand down. I stood tall on the bed as I watched Ben's tongue lick my labia up and down, which turned me on uncontrollably. His tongue was sexy, but seeing my cum on his tongue was even sexier.

Ben spent several minutes underneath me licking my pussy when he said, "My cock is so hard. I need to be inside of you."

I turned my body around, and as I did, cum came out of my pussy. I could feel it running down my leg. I turned my body around and then sat down on Ben's cock. It slid in easily because I was so wet. I moved up and down a couple times and when I looked down I could see my cum covering his cock. It was such a turn on. I moved faster and faster because I was so turned on, but I could tell he was getting turned on faster than me so I said, "Rub my clit."

The distraction for him and extra friction for me might allow us to cum at the same time. Ben took his thumb and moved it in a circular motion around my clit. I concentrated hard because I wanted to cum at the same time as Ben. I wanted to feel his cock pulsate inside of my pussy at the same time I came in order to heighten my orgasm. I wanted a great physical orgasm to wake me up because I didn't want my body to be tired anymore.

I continued moving up and down on Ben's cock and then he said, "I'm going to cum."

I said, "No, you aren't. You aren't going to cum until I tell you to come."

Ben's face looked a little worried, but he held out and when I said, "Cum for me" I felt his cock pulsate right away. While his cock was pulsating inside of me I came and had an orgasm that was heightened in more pleasure than I had experienced in awhile.

After I was finished orgasming, I moved my pussy off Ben's cock and lay down next to him while I caught my breath. Ben was catching his breath, too. With shortened breath Ben said, "That. That is why you should be the boss of the bedroom."

I said, "I'll make a deal with you. If you take care of being the boss of cleaning, I'll be the boss of fucking."

Ben said, "You have yourself a deal, Mrs.

Wright."

The next two days went by fast and the night before the wedding arrived. A group of sixty of us went to dinner together, occupying an entire restaurant. Ben's brother-in-law, Bo, gave a nice speech and then the women and men separated. The men went to the casino while the women all came back to the suite my mother and father had gotten to keep me away from Ben for the night. While all the women were in the suite, room service knocked on the door delivering several bottles of champagne. After the man delivered the champagne, I snuck out the door behind him and handed him a note and a fifty dollar bill. I told him to go find Ben Wright in the casino and give him the note. The man smiled and said, "Yes, ma'am."

I hated when people called me ma'am, but I was glad he understood. I sent Ben a note telling him to meet me on the beach at 1 a.m. sharp. I figured at the rate the women had been drinking they'd all be passed out by then and I could sneak away to have sex with Ben. With everyone telling me I couldn't see Ben until the wedding, it made me want to see him even more.

I enjoyed the night with the women and got more drunk than I had planned on, especially since my wonderful aunt got us a stripper. Sherry looked completely appalled by when the stripper walked into the suite, but once he started dancing she was up dancing with him and "making it rain" dollar bills all around him. I couldn't stop laughing and for the first time I saw Catherine really laughing. She wasn't acting like her usual high strung self. The stripper must've pulled the pole out of her ass.

Once midnight hit I was ready to sneak away to see Ben. One by one, my family and friends left to go to their rooms. Even before Nikki and Bree left, my mother was passed out on the bed, which was perfect for my plan. About twenty minutes before 1 a.m., I quietly snuck out the door and went down to a bar. I asked the bartender to make me a surprise shot and then a glass of champagne before I made my way down to the beach. I was surprised at how dark and quiet the beach was, but luckily when I got down there I spotted Ben. Just one look at him and I could tell he was really drunk. When he saw me he yelled out, "My bride, my boodieful bride, I'm obber here!"

I was drunk, but by the slurs in his words I could tell he was far more drunk than I was. I quickly walked over to the chair Ben was sitting on and crawled on top of him. I said, "I'm so glad you came."

Ben said, "It was a harb get away cause Bo and your fadder had their eyes on me, but I twold them I was gonna go to pee. I did, I did go to pee, and I didn't lie, but when I finished I snuck out a back dwoor."

I smiled and said, "My parents trying to keep us apart was too big of a turn on not to see you."

Ben said, "Oh yeah, baby? I mean babe. I mean darwing."

I felt bad Ben worried so much about calling me "baby" after me yelling at him on New Year's Eve because that's what Chase always called me. I said, "Yes, I want to fuck right here and now on the beach."

Ben's words really slurred when he said, "Oh wah, let's dew sex."

All his slurring told me that fucking was most likely not going to happen, but I wanted to. I wanted to be bad and disobey my mother telling me that I couldn't see Ben on the day of my wedding and I wanted to prove the superstition that it was bad luck for the groom to see the bride on the day of their wedding was wrong.

I unzipped Ben's pants and pulled his cock out through the fly. I pulled my panties to the side and then sat on his semi-hard cock. I moved up and down, working to make his cock harder so I could feel pleasure from it, but it wasn't getting harder. I kept at it though and he seemed to be enjoying it. I looked up from looking at his cute face and looked at the water. I continued to move my body up and down on his cock, but I started feeling like his cock was getting softer instead of harder with each thrust. When I looked back down at Ben, I noticed he had fallen asleep. I couldn't help but laugh. I got off his cock, zipped up his fly, and lay down on the chair next to him.

I decided to let him sleep for a few minutes and enjoy the fresh smell of the sea and the stars in the sky. I sat there for several minutes, enjoying the quiet before waking up Ben so I could walk his drunk ass back to his room. When I woke Ben up, he looked at me with a smile before he said with a slur, "You are beauteous, Aude."

I smiled and laughed a little at his slurring words and how he called me Aude when I said, "You are just drunk."

Ben said with a slur, "No, nooooooo, this man is not drunk."

I said, "Come on non-drunk boy. Let's go back to the room."

Ben asked, "Aude, are we gonna have sex?"

I jokingly said, "Yes, tons of sex."

Ben said, "Aude, you are silly. We can't have the sex till we are married."

I laughed as I said, "You are right. We won't have sex until we are married."

Ben said, "Good cause I don't want your

dad to kong-powy kick my ass."

I kept laughing as I put my hand out to help Ben out of the lounge chair. When he stood up he said, "Whoa, I think planet Earth is moving faster tonight." I laughed at Ben's remark and he continued, "That's not funny. If the Earth's rotation gets messed up, we will die. We can't die because we are getting marrrrrrrrried."

Ben and I walked for a couple minutes when all of a sudden he said, "Look away, my dear!" before bending over and throwing up. I rubbed Ben's back as he threw up on the sand and when he was finished he said while wiping his mouth, "I'm sowwy bout that."

I said, "Don't worry about it. Let's get you back to your room."

Ben asked, "How did I get so wucky to find a girl like you? I mean, I've been such an asshole to so many girls and then I found a cool chick like you. And you actewally like me back!"

I said, "Ben, I love you back."

Ben said, "See, it just keeps getting better!"

As I was putting my key card in the door to Ben's room, Bo opened the door and seemed surprised to see me. Bo asked Ben, "Where did you go?"

Ben said, "I went to have sex with my bride, but I threw up in the sand because the Earth is moving sooooo fast."

Bo laughed before I asked, "How drunk did you get him?"

Bo said, "Hey, a man only gets one bachelor party."

I said, "I better get back to my room before my mother notices I'm gone. Can you take it from here?"

Bo said, "I got it. Thanks for returning him."

Ben said with a slur, "No returns, Aude. We are in this until death."

I said, "I know" as I gave Ben a kiss on the cheek and walked out the door.

The next morning, the morning of my wedding, I woke up to my mother poking me saying, "Audrey, wake up dear. There's a special delivery for you."

I rubbed my eyes as I opened them and two men walked in with carts full of bouquets of white daisies. I sat up and watched as they placed them around my bed. When they left, I laid my head back down on my pillow and closed my eyes. My mother said, "You can't go back to sleep! It's your wedding day."

I said, "Just give me five more minutes, Mom."

As soon as I closed my eyes though, there was another knock on the door. I could hear my mother run over to open it. When she opened the door I heard Bo talk to her on the other end saying, "Here's a little gift for the bride from the groom."

My mother said, "Thank you, Bo. I'll take it to her."

When I heard my mother approaching the bed, I opened my eyes and she handed me a Harry Winston bag. In it was a card that read, "Our time as one starts today." I opened the box inside of the bag and there was a Harry Winston diamond watch. My mother said, "Wow, this man spoils you."

I said, "I'm still getting used to it. I am going to close my eyes for five more minutes."

My mother said, "Come on, Audrey. I'm so excited for today. Wake up, put on this beautiful watch and let's head to the spa."

I said, "Mom, you don't even like fancy diamonds."

My mother said, "I like knowing my girl will be taken care of."

I said, "Is it bad that the gifts are getting a little old?"

My mother said, "Christ, Audrey! Do you have any idea how many women are out there wishing to have a man like Ben? You better start appreciating what you have. Your father and I have rarely ever said anything about your love life, even when you were dating that strange man, Chase, but this time I am not going to let you put off such a wonderful man who only wants to give you the world. Now get out of bed and get dressed because the man you are marrying today and the man I married booked us a morning at the spa."

I knew she wasn't going to let me go back to sleep so I threw the covers off and got out of bed as I said, "Yes, ma'am!"

After getting out of bed and putting some clothes on, my mother and I met the girls down at the spa. After the spa treatments, it was time for hair and makeup. Once I was all dolled up, some of us headed back to my suite to get dressed. My stomach was bothering me a little bit so I waited in my bra and panties while everyone else got dressed. It was probably the mix of champagne at the spa and the Red Bull I had just chugged from feeling tired that was playing tricks on my stomach. After everyone was dressed, I went and sat on the toilet for a few minutes to see if anything would happen. I browsed Facebook while I sat, but nothing was working its way out of my ass. Time was running out so I walked out of the bathroom and Nikki and Bree assisted me into my wedding dress. My mother had tears in her eyes and all I could think was how awkward it was to have half a dozen women watching two girls dress me. On top of that, I had a photographer in my face.

Once I was fully dressed and my mother finished crying, we made our way down to the beach. I watched from afar with my father as people took their seats. While I was standing with my father, I felt my stomach rumble. It began rumbling to a point where I knew that something was about to happen. I slowly released a hot fart and my father commented asking if I had just farted. I told him I had and that I had to go to the bathroom. He asked, "You need to go to the bathroom right now? We need to walk down the aisle in a couple of minutes."

I said, "Stall the wedding. I need to go to the bathroom."

I ran to the nearest bathroom and while I was experiencing explosive diarrhea in a bathroom stall by the resort's pool, I felt bad for the women going in and out of the stall next to me. The noises and smells my ass was making were catastrophic. I also worried about my dress getting wet from the pool water on the bathroom floor. Once I felt like I had emptied out my bowels, I got off the toilet and started walking back to the beach. On my way I heard a familiar voice say, "Audrey, I knew you wouldn't follow through with it."

I stopped in my tracks because I knew that voice all too well. I couldn't believe this was happening. More shit! When I looked to my side, I saw Chase standing and looking at me. I screeched, "What the hell are you doing here?"

Chase said, "I am here for you."

I asked, "Why?"

Chase said, "I knew you wouldn't marry this guy because you are meant to be mine."

I said, "Chase, I just had to use the bathroom. The moment I get back to the beach I will be walking down the aisle."

Chase said, "No, you won't marry him. You

and I are meant for one another. You are meant to be a part of MY movement."

I said, "I want nothing to do with YOUR movement."

Chase put his hand out and said, "Come with me, Audrey."

I said, "No fucking way. What, are you going to tie me to a tree in my wedding dress and bring all your bitches around like you did in the vision you had?"

Chase said, "Audrey, come with me. You know that being with me is where you are meant to be."

I said, "Chase, you need to get the fuck out of here. Don't you have enough girlfriends to annoy?"

Chase said, "You are my chosen one and I am not leaving until you join me on my journey of enlightenment."

I said, "Get the fuck out of here," before turning to walk away.

As I took a step away, Chase grabbed my upper arm hard to pull me toward him as he said, "You are not going anywhere without me."

I yanked my arm hard enough to make Chase let go of me, I saw Ben walking up to us at a fast pace. I didn't know what to say, but I didn't have time to say anything because Ben walked right up to Chase and punched him in the face. Ben threw a wicked punch, which totally turned me on. After taking Ben's punch to the face, Chase said, "I am going to fucking sue you for battery."

Ben said, "Sue me, you crazy man."

As Chase rubbed his cheek he said, "Hand over Audrey. You and I both know she belongs to me."

Ben said, "You have one minute to get off the grounds and out of my sight before I kick the shit out of you. Do you want me to count down from sixty?"

My father stepped in and said, "Chase, if you don't walk away at this moment, I will make sure you spend the next year in a foreign prison."

Chase stood up still holding his cheek when he said, "Expect to hear from my lawyer, Ben, and Audrey, follow me."

I said, "What the fuck is wrong with you, Chase? I am going nowhere with you." I put my hand in Ben's as I said, "You need to leave now."

Chase said, "You are not listening to God's message and he is going to punish you."

Ben let go of my hand and jumped on Chase, pushing him down to the ground. Ben went crazy on him with punches as my father and I tried to break up the fight, but Ben would not stop. Even Bo rushed over and tried to pull them apart. It wasn't until two resort security men came over that Ben and Chase were separated. Chase's face looked beaten up and Ben had a bloody nose. I pulled the handkerchief my mother had made me from a bonnet I wore as a child and put it up to Ben's face to stop the blood that was running out of his nose. When I handed the handkerchief to Ben I said, "I am so sorry about this."

Ben said, "Don't worry about it."

The two security men holding Chase asked me, "What would you like us to do, ma'am?"

My father said, "Place that man behind bars."

I said, "No, just make sure he leaves this resort immediately and is not allowed back."

One of the security men said, "Yes, ma'am."

My father said, "Audrey, he needs a lesson."

I said, "Dad, just let him be escorted out of here so I can enjoy my wedding."

As the two security officials walked Chase away from us my father yelled out, "If you come near my daughter again, I swear it will be the last hour of the day you will ever see."

Hearing my father's threat to Chase was a little shocking. My father never made idle threats. Once Chase was gone I looked at Ben and asked, "Are you sure you still want to marry me?"

Ben wiped his nose with my handkerchief before he pulled me over and kissed me. After the kiss he said, "I would've put that man in foreign jail, but you are kind and that's why I love you. I am going to run to the bathroom to clean up and then I'll be waiting for you at the end of the aisle, my beautiful bride."

I smiled at Ben and said, "I'll be there."

Minutes later I was walking down an aisle of white rose petals and smiling at Ben a smile bigger than I had ever smiled before. I didn't feel nervous in any way. I was ready. I was excited. I was about to marry an amazing man that I had no idea how I was able to score. I reached Ben at the pseudo altar surrounded by every tropical flower imaginable. He gave me a light kiss on the lips, but the minister interrupted our kiss by saying, "Not yet, lovebirds."

Ben pulled away realizing we weren't allowed to kiss until we said 'I do' and wiped my lips with his hand. He said, "Sorry, I shouldn't have kissed you yet."

I smiled at Ben and then we turned to the minister. As the minister spoke to us and our family and friends, I felt like I was having an out of body experience. I was standing next to a man who loved me for exactly who I was. I was about to recite vows that connected me to someone for the rest of my life. I was getting married.

After Ben and I said, 'I do,' the crowd cheered for us and we kissed a long and passionate kiss. A kiss that was probably too passionate for a wedding ceremony, but I didn't care because I loved Ben and I loved expressing my love for him every chance I got. We walked back up the aisle, past our family and friends, and then stopped to kiss again. As Ben kissed

159

me, I felt myself move closer to him. I didn't want our kiss to end. I just wanted to stay in that moment forever. Ben must've been able to feel my pull toward him when we separated because he said, "It's you and me, everyday from now and forever."

I said, "Ben, thank you. Thank you for loving me and thank you for being here with me right now."

Ben said, "Right now and forever."

I softly repeated, "Right now and forever."

After the sunset wedding, there was a candlelit dinner set up for us on the beach. We all ate and drank the many bottles of wine and champagne that were served to us. Ben and I walked to each table to take photos with our family and friends after we ate our food. Once we visited each table, the DJ called us to the makeshift dance floor in the sand for our first dance. Ben took my hand and led me to the dance floor when I heard the song he chose for us start playing. He had chosen *Moon River* by Andy Williams, which was a favorite of mine, especially since it was in *Breakfast at Tiffany's*. As Ben held me close dancing, I realized just how much Ben paid attention to what I loved. Not really knowing me for long, he knew me because he had taken the time to get to know what was important to me.

In my daze of admiration that Ben had chose a song I loved, Ben asked, "What do you think of our song?"

I looked at Ben and said, "I am so glad we are after the same rainbow's end."

Ben said, "I am excited to see the world with you, Mrs. Audrey Wright."

I gave Ben a light kiss on the lips before I said, "Thank you. Thank you for making everything I never thought could be possible for me possible, Mr. Wright."

Holding each other close, Ben and I walked back to our suite after the wedding reception. When we got inside the room we both crashed down on the bed fully clothed. Ben said, "I know we are supposed to have sex on our wedding night, but what if we slept for a couple hours in our clothes and then woke up and had sex. Would it still count? You look amazing and I wish I had enough energy to undress you and pleasure you right now."

I was surprised I felt okay with that. I was exhausted too so I said, "Ben, I love you dearly and I think you are the sexiest man on Earth, but I am one-hundred percent okay with that. Let's just take a quick nap and then fuck."

Ben gave me a kiss on the forehead and said, "I love you."

With my eyes closed and while dozing off, I said, "I love you, too."

Fully dressed in our wedding attire, Ben and I fell asleep cuddled up to one another believing that in just a couple hours we'd wake up in each other's arms ready to fuck for the first time as Mr. and Mrs. Wright. Little did we think we'd sleep until 10 a.m. when my mother would wake us up by pounding on the door to our suite. When I heard the knocking, I scooted my body closer to Ben for warmth as I whispered to Ben, "Someone's at the door."

Ben mumbled something back and I tried to fall back asleep. The knocking continued so I lifted my right arm up to give Ben a smack to wake him up when my arm felt sore. I said, "Ow."

The pain kept me from actually giving a little smack to Ben, but he still woke up and said, "What's wrong? Are you hurt?"

I said, "My upper arm hurts."

Ben sat up quickly and said, "Let me see."

When Ben sat up I said, "That red mark you had on your cheek from the fight yesterday turned black and blue."

Ben said, "Yeah, it really hurts."

I said, "I'm sorry about Chase showing up here and ruining our wedding."

Ben said, "He didn't ruin our wedding. It was the most perfect day for us and our family. I just hope he finally got the message to stay out of our lives."

I said, "Me too. Should we answer the knocking on the door?"

Ben said, "Hold on, let me see where he grabbed you on your arm. Does it really hurt?"

I lifted my arm up and said, "Yeah, it's really sore."

Ben looked at it and said, "Audrey, why

didn't you let us send him to jail? Your arm is black and blue."

I said, "I just worried he would cry like a baby in a foreign jail. He's not much of a tough guy."

Ben said, "Audrey, you need to stop sticking up for him. Look at you arm."

I lifted my arm and as I looked at it, I touched my arm and felt a lump. I said, "Crap, he bruised it so bad that there's a lump."

Ben said, "Nothing except relaxation for us until we heal. Let's get appointments at the spa tonight before we fly to Bali."

I kissed Ben on the cheek and said, "That sounds perfect. Now I think one of us has to open the door for my mother because she's not going to stop knocking until we do."

Ben said, "I'll bet ten bucks my mother is with her."

Ben went and opened the door and it was just my mother. After Ben talked to her, he came back and I said, "You owe me ten bucks."

Ben said, "I'll pay you, but not until I get you out of that wedding gown. We have to be in the lobby in twenty minutes to meet the family, but I am not leaving until I have sex with my bride for the first time as Mrs. Wright."

I said, "Get me out of this gown!"

Ben worked for a good two minutes to get me out of my dress before bending me over the side of the bed and penetrating me from behind. Even though I was tired and would have preferred to be lying on my back enjoying sex, I knew we didn't have much time and doggie style got me off a lot faster. When we started my pussy was dry, but it didn't take long before I felt my pussy get wet. I closed my eyes and concentrated, feeling Ben's cock move in and out of my pussy. I knew it was going to be a quickie, but I wanted it to be a quickie in which I had an orgasm, even if it was a small one. I needed a pick me up.

I took in each thrust and as Ben pushed his hard cock in and out of my pussy I said, "Spank my ass."

Ben did as told and smacked my ass hard, so hard I could feel the burn. I said, "Spank my ass again!" Ben did as told and I could feel myself getting turned on by his control. I said, "Again, harder."

Ben did as I said, but then said, "Spanking you is starting to turn me on too much."

I said, "Hold back your orgasm and keep spanking me until I cum. You are not allowed to cum before me."

Ben continued spanking me and each time he spanked me, he talked more and more dirty. I liked hearing his dirty talk and although his words sounded degrading, I knew how he truly felt about me so they were a turn on. My ass had to have been bright red when I finally came. While I was coming, I felt Ben's cock pulsate inside of my pussy. When Ben's cock finished pulsating, I felt Ben pull out of my pussy before sitting down on the bed next to me. As Ben sat and caught his breath, I remained bent over the side of the bed to catch mine. I said, "It feels good to finally be out of that dress."

Ben said, "You looked amazing in that dress. I think you should wear it more often."

I said, "Only once, buster."

Ben said, "If we got married a million times over, I'd be happy."

I said, "How about next time I wear some lingerie and we have a private wedding?"

Ben said, "I like the way you think. Now we need to go throw on some clothes to go say goodbye to our family and friends."

en and I said goodbye to our family and friends and then relaxed on the beach and at the spa. The next day our jet was back in Punta Cana, ready to take us to Bali. When we got on our jet I couldn't believe I was still feeling tired after our full day of quiet relaxation. I usually hated long flights, but I was on a private jet with a pull out couch that I could sleep on so I looked forward to the hours ahead.

As the flight took off, Ben and I drank our champagne and enjoyed conversing, but once in the air Ben pulled out his laptop and said he wanted to get caught up on work. I told him I was going to take a nap so Ben pulled out the couch bed and the flight attendant brought me out some pillows and blankets. I lay down and closed my eyes. When my eyes were closed, I felt Ben come over and kiss me on the forehead before whispering, "Sleep tight."

Sleep tight I did and I slept for almost twelve hours. When I woke up, Ben was spooning me and holding me tight. I took in his scent, his warmth, his cuddle and I smiled. I was married to a man, a kindhearted, sexy man who truly loved me just the way I was. I lay in Ben's cuddle for awhile and then decided to get up. I sat down in a seat and turned on my computer. While my computer was turning on, I hit the button next to my seat requesting assistance from Frieda, our flight attendant. When Frieda appeared, I asked for a glass of wine and a light snack. She went back up front to retrieve the items and I started sifting through my emails. Most of it was crap, but I responded to an email with questions from my agent. Editing was almost complete for my second memoir, *Time for Audrey Buchanan*. I thought about it for a few moments and realized I was no longer Audrey Buchanan, but I was now Audrey Wright. I liked that, Audrey Wright. Too bad it wasn't spelled 'Write' because that would have been very fitting. Even though I liked the sound of Audrey Wright, I was glad I had six more weeks to be Audrey Buchanan before we were back in the States to make the change legally.

I got up to go to the bathroom before Frieda returned. On my way walking to the rear of the plane there was a tiny bit of turbulence and I fell into the wall. I hit the wall with my right shoulder, which sent some pain shooting through my bruised arm. I shook it off and sat down as Frieda was waiting for me with wine, Doritos, and Nutter Butter cookies. I thanked Frieda for the snack and then she walked back to the front cabin. While I was sipping the wine and munching on junk food, I touched my arm again and could still feel the pain. I went to look at the bruising, but the lights were dim. As I rubbed my arm I could feel the lump inside of my arm. Chase must've grabbed me even harder than I thought because whatever was swollen made for a pretty large lump under the skin of my upper arm.

I shook my head back and forth thinking about how Chase had shown up on my wedding day. I looked over at Ben sleeping and smiled. As I watched him sprawled out on his back snoring away, I thought about how lucky I was to have him. Ben went a little crazy on Chase when Chase showed up at our wedding, but Chase needed a little sense smacked into him. I continued watching Ben sleep for several minutes just appreciating his love and how he made me feel. As I was lost in my feel good moment, Ben let out a snort of a snore before rolling over onto his side and farting really loud. After he farted, he let out a little laugh in his sleep and then started snoring again. I couldn't help but giggle at what I had just witnessed. While giggling, I realized that I found Ben's snort and fart endearing. I had to be truly in love with Ben if a moment like that made me feel happy. I had loved Chase, but not the same way I loved Ben. I was under a spell when I was with Chase. I lived in a fog, per se, where everything was about him. Even the things he did for me were about satisfying his ego. Chase didn't want to build a life with me, he wanted me to participate in whatever character he was morphing himself into at that time. One day he wanted to appear single and the next day he needed me so he could score his reality show. When that didn't work, he felt he needed a harem of women and again, when that wasn't working he needed my name to make it work. He did all this under false pretenses too, appearing that what he was doing was successful when he was actually living off borrowed dimes. Chase's only concern was and is constant attention from others, a condition where no matter how much attention he receives he will never be satisfied.

The love I had for Chase was real to me, but it wasn't a good love and I knew inside I still felt a love for Chase. I still loved Chase, but not in the way I used to love him. My heart still felt for him only because I pitied him. I didn't want to pity Chase anymore because I didn't want to share any bit of my heart with him. I wanted him out of my life so I started to think of ways I could rid myself of him. The likelihood of Chase showing up in London wanting money from me was tiny, but I knew he was desperate. I decided to write an email to my lawyer, Phil, asking him to draw up an agreement of some sort to serve to Chase. The agreement would state that Chase could not contact me or Ben in any way, shape, or form; no phone, no email, no showing up at my home, no social media, no written letters, not even a fax. If Chase signed this agreement, I would front the money he would get for the film.

I sent the email off to Phil and he responded rather quickly that he would come up with a written contract and send it off to Chase, but noted he didn't agree with me fronting Chase the money and that the agreement was really just words and wouldn't hold up in court. I knew it wasn't a totally binding agreement, but hoped it would serve as a message to Chase and fronting the money would at least help clean up some of the trouble he had gotten himself into. I thanked Phil for writing up the agreement and asked him to let me know once the papers had been served to Chase.

I went through some more emails while enjoying my glass of wine. I browsed Facebook and approved dozens of tags of me on my wedding day. I didn't approve the ones I didn't think I looked good in and the one my fucking cousin decided to post of the Ben and Chase showdown. I reported the photo and sent her a message requesting she take it down. What the fuck was wrong with her? Who posts a photo of that?

Once I wasted over an hour and a half on the Internet, I decided to crawl back into bed with Ben. I slowly got into bed and spooned Ben from behind. I heard him say, "Hi honey" as I wrapped my arms and legs around him. Once settled in, I used my left hand to rub his cock from over his mesh pants. With each rub I made, I felt his cock getting harder and harder. Once it felt like I was rubbing a brick, Ben turned around and kissed me. I kissed him back and after a few moments he pulled away and asked, "Can you wake me up like that every day for the rest of our lives?"

I said, "The only other way I'd want to wake you up is by putting your cock in my mouth."

Ben said, "My God, I am a lucky man," as he moved on top of me working to take his pants off.

Once Ben's pants were off, he pulled down my pants and penetrated my pussy. I wished he had done a little warming up first, but with each thrust I felt myself feeling more and more wet. Once he was able to slip and slide inside of me, I felt him move faster and faster. It felt good, but the bar under the pull out couch was digging right into my back. I moved a little to try to get more comfortable, but it kept digging into my back. Ben asked what was the matter and I told him how the bar on the bed was digging into my back. Ben wrapped his arms around my back and pulled me up. I was now sitting on his cock as he sat on the bed. I moved my body up and down, riding his cock and with each movement I made I saw Ben losing himself further and further into my breasts as they bounced in front of his face.

I continued moving up and down on Ben's

cock, but for some reason it wasn't feeling as good as I wanted it to. I said, "I want to stand up and have you fuck me from behind."

Ben obliged and moved me off him quickly before getting off the bed and putting his hand out to assist me off the bed. Once I was standing, we move over by a wall. I bent over and Ben penetrated me from behind. His penetration felt amazing and I knew I had made the right choice by requesting we reposition. He held my hips as he moved his cock in and out of my pussy and with each thrust I felt pleasure. It didn't take long before I said, "Ben, I'm going to cum, hard."

Ben said, "Cum for me, baby, I mean darling. Cum hard. I want to feel your pussy cum on my dick."

I released my orgasm and as I did I heard Ben moan, "Fuck, that feels amazing" as his cock pulsated inside of me. Coming at the same time as Ben made my orgasm so much better. If only we could do that every time we fucked. We were getting there. After we both came we walked over to the bed and lay down. I took a few moments to catch my breath before I said, "Ben, I need to tell you something."

Ben asked, "Is it good or bad?"

I said, "Both."

Ben said, "Alright, tell me."

I said, "While you were sleeping I asked my lawyer, Phil, to draw up an agreement to serve to Chase. The agreement states that he cannot contact you or me in any way, shape, or form."

Ben asked, "Isn't that an order of protection or something?"

I said, "Yeah, sort of. I mean this agreement I had written up isn't totally legally binding, but I am hoping it will serve as something to prevent Chase from contacting either of us."

Ben asked, "Audrey, what else are you not telling me? I can see it in your face. There's something more to this."

I said, "I was getting to that."

Ben said, "Okay, then tell me."

I said, "I told Phil if Chase signed the agreement I would front the money he will get for the movie rights. I love you, Ben. I love you so much and I don't want him in our lives anymore. If I give him the money then he can start to clean up his mess and stay out of our lives."

Ben said, "I know you still love him, Audrey, but I also know you don't love him the way you love me. I just wish you would let him go."

I said, "I have when it comes to being in love with him, but I still pity him. I feel so sorry for him."

Ben asked, "Why?"

I said, "I realized that Chase is insecure."

Ben mumbled, "I could have told you that the moment I read your memoir *Dating Chase Walker*."

I said, "I see it now. When I first met him I

thought he was a man who had it all together, but as I got to know him I realized he is a man who doesn't love himself."

Ben said, "There is nothing sadder."

I said, "Ben, I don't love Chase in a way that would ever threaten our love. I want you to know that."

Ben said, "I know and I've known that since the day you attempted sex with me while you were in New York. I don't feel threatened by Chase, but I don't like the way he takes advantage of you."

"I know and I feel giving him the money so he can go off and do whatever he needs to do to satisfy his ego will keep him out of our lives."

"My opinion is that by giving Chase the money you are enabling Chase's delusion and he will be back as soon as that money runs out, but if you honestly feel that is what needs to be done, I support you. I don't want our money in his hands, but I also trust that you know what's best for you. So, if fronting that money to him is what you want to do, I will support it."

I said, "Thank you. I just want him out of our lives and I think this is our answer."

Ben didn't look convinced, but responded, "Alright."

After a few moments of silence passed, I said, "Ben?"

Ben said, "Yes, my dear."

I asked, "How does one transfer hundreds of thousands of dollars? I mean, if you give over ten thousand dollars do you get taxed on it?"

Ben said, "I'll take care of it. How about I handle this Chase situation from here?"

I asked, "What do you mean? I want it to be taken out of my money, not yours."

Ben said, "It's our money now. Let me handle this going forward. I don't want you to have to worry about him anymore. I will have the money and document taken care of."

I said, "Okay, but I'd like to learn how this is done and it has to be money taken from my account, not yours."

Ben said, "Audrey, our accounts are one now."

I said, "Not until we get back into the States in six weeks."

Ben said, "True. Alright, we are going to do this together. Everything that happens with this will be a team decision."

I said, "Everything in our lives going forward will be a team decision."

Ben smiled at me and said, "I am so lucky to have picked a great teammate."

I said, "Me too" before I gave him a kiss on the cheek.

Ben and I landed in Bali and we had sex on every square inch of our bungalow. We even fucked on the see through glass where I could see fish swimming by on the living room floor and under a waterfall on one of our private excursions. After Bali, we flew to London and it felt like the moment we landed Ben was immersed in work. I didn't mind though, I was almost grateful. I slept until noon and then picked a different direction to walk in after walking out the door of our flat every day. I would just walk to wherever my feet took me, not worrying if I got lost and ignoring how tired my body felt. I ended up at chapels, Big Ben, Trafalgar Square, Buckingham Palace, museums, shopping, Palace of Westminster, parks, aquariums, and more. I just walked and if I came across a stop for the Underground train system, I'd get on it and get off at a random stop. There were a few days I had to meet Ben for business lunches and dinners with other investors and partners, but most of the time I was on my own.

A couple weeks passed in London and the only thing I was writing were journal entries. I was too intrigued by my surroundings. I kept telling myself I needed to sit down and write a story, but I couldn't help but feel the need to get out and soak in everything that was around me. One day Ben came home after a meeting and said to me, "Let's go to Paris tomorrow."

I thought to myself: *I had married a man who just randomly said that we should go to Paris the next day. I was by far the luckiest woman in the world.* I clapped my hands and said, "Let's do it!"

Ben said, "We can get a villa for a few days in the south of France after we visit Paris, too."

Was I in dreamland? Was this really my new reality? It was my new life with Ben because the next morning we went to the airport and we were on our way to Paris. We checked into the Four Seasons George V, Paris and I never wanted to leave the hotel. Never! It was so beautiful. Our bathroom had gold faucets. Gold faucets! As I stood in the bathroom admiring the décor, I said, "Ben, come here."

Ben walked into the bathroom and asked, "Yes, my dear."

I said, "Ben, there are fucking gold faucets in this bathroom."

Ben laughed a little before he said, "Do you like gold faucets?"

I said, "Ben, I don't think you are comprehending how utterly fascinating this is to me. We need to have sex in here right now while I hold onto one of these gold faucets."

Ben said, "If you really love gold faucets, we can have them in our house."

As I took my shirt off I said, "Drop your pants right now and come have sex with me while I hold this gold faucet."

Ben's pants fell to the ground and he walked over by me. He said, "I know this gold faucet is turning you on, but you might have to warm me up a little bit because the gold faucet isn't doing the same thing for me."

I got down on my knees and put Ben's cock in my mouth. As I was moving his cock in and out of my mouth Ben handed me a towel and said, "I'm a gentleman so here's a towel for you to kneel on."

I took the towel and put it under my knees while I kept his cock in my mouth. I used both hands to pleasure his cock along with my mouth; my right hand caressing his balls lightly and my left hand holding his shaft tightly. I moved my mouth in and out for a few minutes and when I felt his cock was nice and hard I stood up and kissed Ben. After our kiss he said, "You give the best head."

I said, "And you fuck me just right so I am going to turn around and grab this faucet while you penetrate me."

Ben said, "Wait, let me kiss you one more time just because you make me so happy."

I smiled as Ben kissed me and then I turned around and grabbed the faucet. It was a very odd fascination to want to get fucked while holding a gold faucet, but I think it was more than just the actual faucet turning me on. It was that I was in Paris in a beautiful hotel with décor I only wished I could afford to decorate my apartment with. On top of that, I was with a sexy man who loved me and I was still trying to understand why he loved me so much.

Ben moved his cock in and out of my pussy from behind as I held the faucet. He said, "I can see your cum on my cock and it looks so hot. Look in the mirror, darling, and you will be able to see my cock with your cum on it."

I looked over in the mirror and I saw Ben's sexy body. His hands were holding my hips to guide his cock in and out of my pussy. When I saw his cock move out of my pussy, I could see my cum covering his cock and it turned me on even more. I said, "Faster, fuck me faster."

Ben obliged and moved his cock in and out faster. He said, "Fuck, you are wet. My cock is slipping and sliding in and out of your pussy."

I thought how "slipping and sliding" wasn't the most sexy thing I'd ever heard, but I did find it humorous. I said, "I'm going to cum. I want to cum with you."

Ben said, "I could have cum while your mouth was on my cock. I've just been waiting on you."

I said, "Alright, one, two, three, release."

As I came so did Ben and it felt amazing. Fuck, it was a great orgasm. I knew that gold faucet had special powers. After we came, we sat on the bathroom floor for a few moments catching our breath and coming down from our orgasm highs. Ben said, "Audrey..."

I said, "Yes, Ben?"

Ben said, "I know you said you got that lump in your right breast checked out and they said it was nothing, but it is getting larger. I think you should get a second opinion."

I said, "I never got it checked out. I didn't have time to visit a doctor before we left." I put my hand on my breast and it did feel like it was getting larger, but I lied by saying, "I don't think it's getting larger."

Ben said, "I asked you on the jet on the way to Punta Cana if you got it checked out and you said you did."

I said, "No, you didn't."

He said, "I did and you said it was okay."

I said, "No, I didn't. I'm sure it's fine. Fake boobs feel weird. I will go to the doctor when we return to the States to ease your mind, but I'm positive it is nothing."

Ben said, "I'm going with you."

I said, "Ben, what happens between me and my gynecologist is between him and me."

Ben said, "What? No, when my baby is in your belly I want to be there for every appointment."

I said, "Until there is a thing growing in my vagina, you are not coming with me to see what happens there. It is not pleasant."

"Audrey, I'd feel better if I am there with you to make sure everything is okay."

"Everything will be fine. It probably just feels weird from my implants. I'm due for my annual tune up soon so I'll go once we get back to Chicago. Now let's forget this serious talk and go see Paris!"

Ben and I headed out and went all over Paris like regular tourists. We ended our night at Le Meurice for dinner and had more than our fair share of food and wine. When we got back into our room at the Four Seasons, Ben got on the phone and requested room service to bring us champagne as soon as possible. While he was on the phone, I drunkenly walked into the bathroom and started filling up the bathtub again, fascinated by the gold faucet. Once the tub was full of water and bubbles, I walked out of the bathroom and said, "Monsieur, our bubbles await."

Ben held his hand out and said, "Madam, may I have this dance," as he turned on a song on the iPad with his other hand.

Moon River by Andy Williams began playing. I smiled and walked over by Ben, taking his hand and accepting a dance. We danced for a few moments before Ben said, "Hold on. You are naked so I should be naked, too." Ben took off his clothing quickly and then took my hand to dance again. We moved slowly around the room. Ben whispered in my ear asking, "Are you ready to see the world with me?"

I responded using the lyrics, "Wherever you're going, I'm going your way."

The rest of the song we danced in silence and for some reason I felt like crying. I was overwhelmed with happiness. Ben had brought me into a world I only thought I could dream of. It was like I was living the best book I had could ever write and maybe that's what my grandmother was trying to tell me the night of my bridal shower.

Right after the song ended there was a knock on the door. It was room service with our champagne. We threw on some robes and a man brought our champagne in. He popped the bottle of champagne for us and poured us each a glass before leaving. Once he was gone, Ben and I took our glasses of champagne and went into the bathroom. We got into the bathtub filled with water from the gold faucet and relaxed. Ben asked, "What's our plan for life?"

I said, "That's one big ass general question."

Ben said, "Well, wife, I am just curious as to what we want to do next. What happens when we get back to Chicago and move into our big warehouse of a house?"

I said, "We decorate our new home and entertain. My PR agent Steven wants us to be a part of some reality show on Bravo."

Ben said, "Shh, listen."

I was quiet listening for whatever it was that Ben was having me listen to when I heard

Ben fart. I then felt the bubbles from his fart run up my back. It was utterly disgusting, making it absolutely hilarious. We laughed for a few moments and Ben said, "I knew you'd get a kick out of that."

I said, "Bathtub farts are the funniest farts."

Ben said, "Okay, back to our serious conversation, a reality show?"

I said, "Yeah, apparently it is about Chicago social living and he thinks we'd make a great couple on there."

Ben asked, "Why? Because we have money and you write about sex?"

I said, "I don't know. I don't really want to do it."

Ben said, "If you don't want to do it, then don't. I'd rather not be on a reality show, but if it is something you really want, I will do it."

I said, "I actually don't want to be on one either. It brings back bad memories, but the only reason I would do it is to help my writing career."

Ben said, "You are a success. You don't need a reality show to prove to people you are a success. People on reality shows are usually insecure and in need of attention."

"I know what you mean."

"So you know I am talking about Chase."

"Ben! Why do you have to bring his name up?"

Ben said, "I'm sorry. I know you aren't in

love with him anymore, but it's just that sometimes it is hard. He's fucking everywhere with what is going on."

I said, "It's still weird for me to hear you swear outside of sex."

Ben said, "Sorry, I shouldn't swear."

I said, "No, I find it sexy."

Ben asked, "Oh, really?"

I turned around to kiss Ben as I said, "Yes, really. Swear again."

Ben said, "I want to feel your fucking pussy on my cock right now."

I said, "Say that again."

Ben said, "I want my fucking cock inside of your pussy right now!"

I stood up with bubbles covering my body and put my hand out to assist Ben up. After he got up, we walked out of the bathtub with bubbles still covering our bodies. In the bathroom still, Ben said, "No, let's take our wet bodies to the bed."

I said, "Oh, but the gold faucet turns me on so."

Ben said, "No, I want to be on top. I want to see your beautiful face when I fuck you."

I said, "Swear again. Swear as many times as you can until we get to the bed."

Ben spit out swear word after swear word as we walked to the bed and I felt more and more turned on with each word he said. I don't know why his swearing turned me on, but it did. Maybe it was because it felt like it was out of his element and he was doing it to please me. I could feel my pussy getting more wet with each word he said. When we got to the bed, Ben assisted me on it and I lay down on my back. I still had bubbles all over my body but I didn't care and he didn't seem to either. Once on my back, Ben penetrated my pussy. After his cock was fully inside of me he said, "Audrey, I love you and I am so happy you accepted my proposal to spend the rest of your life with me."

I said, "Ben, I have never felt happier in my life. Thank you for choosing me and for swearing to turn me on even though I know you don't like to swear."

Ben said, "Swearing is growing on me, my gorgeous little bitch."

I laughed and guided Ben's face down to mine to kiss me. When I did, I felt his cock come out of my pussy. As we kissed, I felt so much happiness inside. I could literally feel it in my body. I didn't feel little butterflies inside, but I felt pure happiness running through my body. I stopped for a moment with our lips almost touching and said, "I really love you, Ben, and I have never been happier."

Ben put his forehead on mine and smiled as he said, "Good. I plan to make you feel happier and happier with each day that passes. Whatever it is that you want, I've got it."

I said, "I want your penis inside of me."

Ben slowly pushed his cock back inside of my pussy as he said, "You've got it. What else can I do for you?"

I said, "Push your cock in me deeper."

Slowly, Ben pushed his cock deeper inside of my pussy, as deep as he could push it. With each thrust deep inside of me I felt pleasure. He kept at it, slow for a few minutes and watching him work his cock turned me on. After a few minutes I said, "Stay deep, stay as deep as you can and fuck me hard."

Using many deep small movements, Ben kept at it hitting my deep G spot head on. I liked being fucked deep and felt my pussy tightly grabbing his cock. I knew that as my pussy got tighter, Ben got more and more turned on. I lightly pushed Ben off me and turned around getting on all fours, allowing for a little break for Ben and positioning me to cum fast. Ben penetrated me from behind and moved his cock in and out of my pussy fast. I said, "Spank me!"

Ben gave me a slight slap on the ass, but it wasn't enough. I said, "Spank me again!"

Ben slapped my ass again harder, but again it wasn't hard enough. I said, "Harder!"

Ben slapped my ass again and again, harder and harder while he penetrated my pussy from behind. With each thrust inside of me and his control by spanking me, I finally felt my pussy get tight enough to release an orgasm. I said, "I'm going to cum!"

Ben said, "Cum with me" and a few moments later I felt his cock begin pulsating inside of my pussy so I released my orgasm.

We sat connected by our privates for a few moments, enjoying our orgasms, but then separated and recovered from the ecstasy. As we were coming down I said, "Ben, I love you and I can't believe how much you have given me."

Ben said, "There's so much more to come. Let me keep giving to you."

I was out of breath when I said, "You've given me so much. Let me give to you. How can I give to you?"

Ben said, "Just be here. Be with me. I am happy just being near you."

I said, "Alright, if that's really what you want."

Ben and I arrived back in Chicago and although I loved spring in Chicago, I was sad to be back. I loved being in Europe. There was so much adventure every moment. We arrived back and got to my small apartment. I felt comfort being there, but knew that the comfort I felt wouldn't last because in the next few days we would be viewing our newly remodeled warehouse home. I told Ben I was going to draw a bath after our long trip and Ben said he was going to run to the grocery store to get some food. I kissed Ben goodbye and turned on the bath water. Ben and I had just had sex a thousand times since we had gotten married, but I couldn't help but feel the need to spend some time with my vibrator.

As soon as Ben was out the door, I took my vibrator out of my bottom drawer and blew the dust off it before taking it into the bathroom. I stepped into the warm water and relaxed for a few moments and I couldn't help but think about how much my life had changed in the past few months. Lost in my thought, I caught myself and told myself I couldn't think about life anymore and I needed to get sexy with myself. I had a lot of time with a man, an amazing man, over the past few months so I decided to think about being with a woman. I came up with a scenario in my head where I was on the beach and a woman approached me. It was sunset and there was nobody else on the beach when she came up to me asking if she could sit on the chair next to me. I answered her telling her that she could, but instead she straddled her legs over me before moving in to kiss me. I kissed her back before her hands moved over my breasts. As her hands moved over my breasts, she strategically moved my bikini top to the side exposing my nipples. The cool breeze on them made them hard.

The unknown woman then moved her lips from my lips down my chest, licking my hard nipples. I watched as she licked them and smiled at me, getting turned on more and more with each tongue movement. After spending a few moments on my breasts, the woman moved her way down to my pussy and that's when I turned up my vibrator to high. In my head I could see her looking at me using her tongue to pleasure me while I could feel my vibrator sending pulsating pleasure through my pussy and body. My eyes were closed and my imagination kept going while my vibrator did all the work. Since I hadn't masturbated in a long time, I came fast and hard. Really hard. I yelled out, "Oh yeah" like I was the fucking Kool-Aid man as my pussy pulsated.

When my orgasm finished, I turned off my vibrator and dropped it outside of the bathtub while I sat and enjoyed my orgasm high in the warm water. I could feel the cum exiting my pussy as I sat and it felt good to experience some alone time. I loved Ben, I did, but being in love with someone didn't mean I couldn't spend time loving myself. I sat in the water for a little while and then washed my face before getting out of the bathtub. When I got out and I was drying off, a glob of cum exited and was hanging out of my pussy. I let out a little laugh and then wiped it off with a towel.

After wiping the cum off my pussy, I dried off my body and as I rubbed the towel over my ass I felt that the zit on my ass had gotten bigger. When we left London it was just a little one, but all the sitting and traveling must've made it ripe and nearing ready for popping. I turned around to look in the mirror at the zit on my ass to see how noticeable it was and I saw it had gotten huge. I could see it was ready to be popped so I reached my arm around to pop it when Ben knocked on the bathroom door. He asked, "Audrey, can I come in? I really have to pee."

I said, "Sure" as I picked up the towel off the ground to cover my naked body.

As Ben was peeing he asked, "How was your bath?"

I said, "Good."

Ben continued peeing as he kicked the

vibrator on the floor toward me and asked, "Were you masturbating?"

I said, "I was."

Ben said, "You are one horny girl. We've had sex at least a thousand times since we've been married. Is there something more I should be doing to keep you satisfied?"

As Ben shook his dick a little after he finished peeing I said, "It's not that. We have great sex and I am completely satisfied. Sometimes a girl just needs a little alone time. I'm sure you've masturbated since we got married."

Ben said, "No, you wear me out. Okay, wait actually I did once in the shower."

I said, "See, it's okay to masturbate."

Ben washed his hands as he said, "I see your point. Are you all finished in here? I got some stuff to cook us up something to eat."

I said, "I'll be out in a few. I need to take care of some things first."

Ben asked, "I don't know how women spend so much time in the bathroom. What do you guys do in here for so long?"

I said, "It's embarrassing."

Ben asked, "What, are you tweezing out hairs?"

I said, "No, but I probably should clean up my eyebrows. I do gross things in here."

Ben said, "Oh, I see. You have to poop. I'll leave you in peace then."

I said, "No, I don't have to poop. I have to

pop a zit on my ass."

Ben laughed and asked, "Did you just say you are going to pop a zit on your ass?"

I looked down in embarrassment and said, "Yes, it's huge and gross."

Ben said, "Let me see."

I said, "No way. You don't even like it when I fart. I don't want you down by my asshole."

Ben said, "I won't look at your asshole, although I have seen it when we've had sex doggy style. I'll just look at the zit. I actually like popping zits."

I said, "Gross, really? I'm super disgusting, but I don't even like popping zits."

Ben said, "I love you and it's a weird fascination of mine. Let me see it."

I dropped my towel and bent over. I said, "Don't judge me for this zit. I'm not sure where it came from."

Ben said, "It's a good one" as his fingers moved over it and he popped it.

I asked, "Is this what married life is like? Popping each other's ass zits?"

Ben said, "Love is blind, my darling, and popping a huge zit on your ass didn't make me love you any less" before he kissed me.

I said, "Thank you for popping my zit."

Ben said, "No problem. Now, I am going to make us some food, after I wash my hands of course."

Ben left and I took some more time in the bathroom, tweezing out random hairs and primping myself to a little decency before I walked out. Once I had taken care of the hairs on my face and made myself presentable, I went out to the kitchen. Ben was cooking up something that smelled delicious. He stepped away from the stove for a moment and handed me a glass of wine. I took it and went to sit down at the kitchen table. After I sat down I asked if I could help with anything, but knew it was a rhetorical question because Ben enjoyed handling things in the kitchen. He told me just to relax and that's what I did. As I drank my wine Ben asked, "Audrey, can we try something out tonight?"

I said, "Yes, of course. I love trying new things."

Ben said, "Okay, I think it would be fun to watch a porno together."

I stood up, walked over to Ben, and said, "I thought you'd never ask."

Ben said, "My God, I love you and your sexy dirty mind."

After Ben and I ate, we relaxed for a little while. Ben seemed excited about us watching a porno because he asked if it was time to watch it yet. I said, "Yes, it's time. Why are you so anxious?"

Ben said, "I'm not anxious. I guess because you just masturbated I'm feeling more turned on and wanting to satisfy you."

I said, "Oh, I like keeping you on your toes, but just because I masturbated doesn't mean I don't want to get fucked."

Ben told me to hold on a minute so I stayed in the kitchen sipping on wine and browsing various apps on my phone. When he told me to come into the bedroom I did and it was lit with candles. I walked in with a smile, seeing the set up. He asked me to sit on the bed and I did as told. I sat down, but then he insisted I get comfortable so I did. I pulled the blanket over me and sat sipping my wine. Ben walked over to his side of the bed and crawled under the covers with me. He then grabbed the iPad off the nightstand and turned it on. He asked, "What kind of porno video do you want to watch? Should we pick a category?"

I said, "I'm feeling lucky. Let's browse the new videos."

Ben said, "Sounds good."

Ben and I came across a video titled *She Does it Backwards*, which I immediately thought how backwards was not a word and it should be backward, but it was porn so I had to let it slide. I pointed to the "backwards" porn and said, "Let's watch this one."

Ben clicked on the video and the storyline started rolling. It was terrible, absolutely horrendous and there was no way either of us would ever get turned on by what was going on. I said, "Next."

Ben turned off the video and got back to browsing for several pages when we spotted a video called *Handcock* with a photo of the infamous Hancock building in Chicago and a girl looking like she was giving a hand job. Ben said, "We have to watch this since it is Chicago-based."

I agreed and Ben clicked on the video. It started with some cheesy music and images of the Hancock building, but moved into an office scene. Our eyes were peeled as we wondered what was about to happen when two women walked into the office. Ben said, "Things are about to get interesting."

The two women walked into the office laughing and then one sat on the desk asking the other if she thought their boss would be back soon. The other one's acting skills were not very good when she responded that she didn't know when their boss would be back, but that they should take advantage of their time without him. The one sitting on the desk agreed and they started kissing and undressing one another. This lasted a few moments until the door to the office opened and when it did my eyes widened. I looked over at Ben and he said, "Seriously, what the hell?"

I said, "I don't know."

Ben said, "Fuck! This fucking guy is every-fucking-where!"

Ben swearing outside of his cock being inside of me was not good. He was swearing for good reason though. Chase was the man that walked into the office with the women in the porno. I said, "I had no idea he was doing porn."

Ben said, "I know you didn't, but I feel like we are never going to get away from this guy. He just keeps showing up at all the wrong times."

I said, "I'm sorry about my ex. I know he's a bit out there."

Ben said, "It's not your fault and I don't want to be jealous, but he just really gets on my nerves."

I said, "Don't let him. Let's move on and watch another video."

Ben said, "I want to pleasure you badly, but I am totally turned off right now. There's no way I can have sex. I know you still love him in some sort of way so it drives me crazy when I hear his name or see him."

I said, "Ben, you are right I do still feel for him, but it's in a way in which nobody would ever want another to feel for them. I pity him. I feel bad for him."

Ben said, "I know that and that's what worries me. It's the kind of feeling that makes you want to help someone."

I said, "I have zero desire to ever help Chase anymore and that's why I had that contract drawn up. I do, however, hope he realizes he doesn't have to keep pretending to be someone else to make it in this world."

Ben said, "And what if he realizes this? Are you going to leave me for him because he suddenly discovers he's insecure and he gets his shit together?"

Ben swore again and that meant I hadn't made any progress in calming him down. I kissed Ben gently before I said, "No, Ben, nothing could ever take me away from you. I don't want Chase, I want you. You are the man for me. There is nobody better. I may still love Chase out of sorrow, but I love you in a way in which I could never love another man. I would rid of Chase in a second if I could to make you happy."

Ben said, "Audrey, I know you love me, I do, and I am so sorry I am acting like this right now. I'm just so aggravated with him appearing in our lives at the worst moments."

I said, "Ben, don't be sorry. I realize you walked into a weird situation with me, but I'm asking you to never doubt my love for you. You and I have decades of happiness in front of us and in a couple years we will look back at this moment and laugh. I know the real Chase, who he is when he isn't off acting in desperation. He is a good man, but Ben, oh Ben, there is no man more perfect for me than you. You have made me the happiest girl in the world and I can't wait for the amazing years we have ahead."

Ben said, "That, that right there is why I love you."

I said, "Good because I love you, too. How about we turn off this iPad and go to sleep? We can clear our minds and you can wake me up with your cock in my pussy or in my face. I'll leave that up to you."

Ben laughed a little before he pulled me over to spoon me. He kissed the back of my head before he said, "I love you more than life itself."

I smiled as I scooted my body as close to his as possible and then closed my eyes. I said, "Thank you for choosing me, Ben.

Ben said, "I love you, Audrey."

I said, "I love you, too."

A couple days passed and then we were off to see our new home fully built out with most of our furniture in it. Ben was ecstatic about seeing it so he woke me up early in the morning to head over there. When I woke up though, I wasn't feeling well. I felt very tired and lightheaded. I figured it was just the onset of my period. Ben stood next to the bed showered and ready to get moving when I said, "Ben, can we go tomorrow? I am not feeling very well."

Ben asked, "What's wrong?"

I said, "I'm not sure? I think it's the onset of my period. I am feeling very weak and lightheaded."

Ben said, "I'm starting to worry about you, Audrey. You feel tired a lot and this isn't the first time you've felt lightheaded. I think it's time you see a doctor."

I said, "I'm fine. I'm sure it's just all the changes getting to me. It's all so exciting and love is a great weight loss tool."

Ben said, "I love you more than me and I've gained eight pounds since we started dating."

I said, "No, you haven't. I love you more

and you are just as hot as you were when I visited you in New York for the first time."

Ben said, "No, really. Once we move into our new place we will have more of a schedule so I can work out, but anyway, I think it's time to see a doctor. You still haven't gotten that lump in your breast checked out. That needs to be made a priority. If not for you, for me."

I said, "Alright, I'll go see my gynecologist."

Not feeling well, I still got up and showered. I did want to see our new place and what the interior decorator did with all the random expensive shit I had bought online. We hailed a cab and arrived at our new address. When we pulled up the decorator was outside waiting for us, excited to take us inside and show us what she had done with the place. When we walked in, I was amazed at how everything looked. It was perfect. We walked around, happy with our new home, but when we got into my office I started crying. Ben had all my books from my spare room sent over to our new home and placed on shelves in a room that not only looked, but smelled like an old library. It was the perfect place to write. Although my hundreds of books didn't fill all the shelves, Ben said he knew with time the shelves would be filled with books that I loved.

I kissed Ben and when I did, the interior decorator walked out of the room to give us privacy. After she was gone I whispered in Ben's ear, "I want to fuck in this room right now."

Ben said, "We can't, not just yet. I have another surprise for you."

I asked, "How could you possibly have another surprise for me?"

Ben said, "Darling, you have many years of surprises ahead of you. All I want to do with my life is to make you happy."

I had loved every surprise Ben had given me so far so I was excited to see what he had in store. I took his hand and he led me to the back of our home, but stopped before he opened the door to our garage. He asked if I was ready and I said, "Yes!" with enthusiasm.

Ben opened the door to the garage and when I looked into the garage, there was a Porsche SUV and a Bentley. Ben smiled at me as he said, "You now have a car and I have a SUV. Do you like them?"

I did like his choices in vehicles, but I felt a little upset. I had told him I wanted to buy myself a car with my money. I knew I shouldn't be upset about a man handing me things I never thought I could afford, but he had done so much and I was proud of my earnings. I wanted to buy myself a car. I said, "Ben, I love the cars, but I wanted to be able to buy myself a car with my own money."

Ben said, "But my money is your money."

I said, "I know you say that, but buying myself a car is something I wanted to do."

Ben said, "I'm sorry. I just wanted to do

something nice for you."

I said, "I know, but you keep doing all these crazy amazing things for me. I mean, I am living a life that most girls only dream of. It's a dream so big in which I couldn't even have fathomed meeting a man who would do so much. I love the car, I do, but from here on out I want to be able to do things for myself. Buy me flowers or donuts if you have the urge to buy me things. All other things, let's discuss and do as a couple going forward. I want to be able to participate in decisions like this."

Ben said, "I understand, but please don't be mad."

I said, "Ben, you bought me a Bentley, how could I be mad?"

Ben asked, "So you like it?"

I said, "I fucking love it! But no more buying me things like this."

Ben said, "Got it. Now, do you want to fuck in your car or mine?"

I said, "Yours, it has more room."

Ben grabbed my hand and we walked quickly over to the Porsche. He opened the door and it smelled of new car. I couldn't believe how nice it was inside. We got inside and played with a few gadgets and turned on some sexy music before crawling into the backseat and getting naked. Although there was plenty of room for sitting, it wasn't easy taking our clothes off in the backseat. We both laughed as we uncomfortably pulled off our jeans. Once we were both naked, Ben and I gave each other a look that said we were ready to go. Ben pulled my body toward him and said, "Come here, you beautiful thing."

We kissed for a few moments while Ben's fingers gently rubbed over my pussy and my hand grasped his cock, rubbing it up and down. Car sex wasn't about good foreplay, though, so I moved my body and crawled between the front two seats. Ben adjusted his body so he was sitting on the middle seat of the back seat while the front half of my body was in the front. My back was to him with my legs spread so Ben could penetrate my pussy from behind. Ben said, "Fuck, Audrey, this is the hottest thing I have ever seen. You are wide open to me."

I said, "Lick it or stick it. I'm ready."

Ben lifted my hips a little bit and put his tongue on my pussy for a few moments. I was happy with his decision to do so. I loved feeling his tongue move around my labia. He only licked my pussy for a few moments before guiding my hips down to penetrate his cock. I repositioned so I could move up and down on his cock as fast as possible and once I was positioned just right, I bounced my hips up and down. Ben said, "Fuck, I thought staring at your ass was the hottest thing I have ever seen, but watching it bounce up and down is even hotter. Shit, you know how to work it."

I loved his compliment and hearing his clean mouth swear always turned me on. I kept moving my hips up and down on Ben's cock while being bent over the space leading to the front seat. It was an easy position to maneuver in and it didn't take long before I felt Ben orgasm and cum inside of me. I loved feeling him cum and knowing I could pleasure him, but I wished I had been turned on enough to cum myself. Once I felt Ben's cock stop pulsating, I lifted my pussy off his cock and sat down on the back seat. Ben took a few moments to catch his breath before we decided to get out of the car. After I got out, Ben started laughing when he saw a smear of cum from my pussy left on the seat. He said, "I hope this doesn't stain the leather."

I said, "I hope it does so that every time you look in your back seat you think of me."

Ben laughed as he wiped the cum off the seat with his underwear and then got out of the car. He threw the cum stained underwear on the floor of the backseat and went commando the rest of the day. We walked around our new warehouse of a house for a little while longer and then took his Porsche back to my apartment. When we walked inside, I realized why Ben was so anxious to move into our new place because my apartment was extremely small compared to where we were moving. I'm pretty sure my new library was bigger than my entire apartment.

We used the next few days to pack up and move into our new place. We moved everything out except my mattress and some blankets because I had asked Ben if I could spend one last night there alone. He seemed confused and a little sad that I wanted to spend a night away from him, but I assured him it had nothing to do with him. I had lived in that apartment for many years and wanted to have a one-on-one goodbye with it. Ben kissed me before he left and said to call him when I woke up so he could come pick me up.

The moment he left I took off my clothes. I walked around naked while Ben was home all the time, but there was nothing like being naked while alone. When you are alone, you can sit in ways that aren't flattering and farts never have to be excused. I poured myself a glass of wine and went into my bedroom to sit on the mattress on the floor. I looked around my empty room and as I did I felt a little lump in my throat begin to form. Soon, tears followed. I wasn't sad, I was far from sad. I was so happy about the new direction of my life and loved Ben like I had never loved another, but it didn't mean I wasn't sad to leave a place I had called home for so many years.

After a little dramatic cry, I sipped on my wine and pulled over my computer. I knew I wrote best when I was sad and tonight was the perfect recipe for a good story. I decided to pick up where I had left off on the second book in my memoir series. I hoped I'd never be in a position to be sad as the result of heartache from Ben in the future, so I needed to use this sad opportunity of change to inspire my story. I thought about all that had happened in such a short period of time and started writing from the last book's ending when Ben didn't show up at the Empire State Building.

I refilled my glass of wine and wrote and wrote for a few hours before stopping for a break. I had hid my vibrator in my purse when Ben left so I pulled it out and decided to take a "bate break." I hopped onto PornHub.com to find something to get me going when I remembered Chase had a porno on the website called *Handcock*. I decided to search for it and watch it out of curiosity. I knew it wasn't something I should be watching and it was a total buzzkill when it came on while I was with Ben, but I wanted to see it for myself. It came up on the search and I clicked on it to watch. The scene began playing out with the two girls and then Chase appeared. As I watched I couldn't believe that just a year prior he had sent so much sexual inspiration through my body, but now when I looked at the same person and the same big cock all I could think of was how sorry I felt for him.

When I met Chase I thought of him as this confident man who was trying to change the way men dated; a man who had something to teach. When I started to get to know him I believed that was who he was, but with time I learned he was the most insecure man I had ever met. A man who paid others money he didn't have to get attention, a man who did things to shock people for attention, a man who lived his life as a persona because he longed so badly to be loved. As I watched the porno more, I watched him as he fucked who I recognized as one of his girlfriends, Vivian. As he was penetrating her, he was looking at the blonde girl and I noticed I started shaking my head back and forth. It wasn't a bad shake of the head though; it was more like a shake of gratitude. As I continued watching, my head moved from shaking back and forth to up and down. I had realized not only did my heart feel more warm for Ben by watching this video, but that Chase had found what he needed. I had given Chase every bit of my heart. I was not only infatuated with him, but I loved him dearly. My love, however, could never be enough to satisfy him. I could give him all the attention in the world and sex all day long, but he needed more.

I started smiling as my head shook up and down in happiness for Chase. He had met his match. He had met a woman that was secure or insecure enough to allow Chase to find himself; a woman who didn't mind sharing her man. Chase had moved into a strange phase in his life, but who was I to judge what he was doing. Yes, his words and showing up randomly scared and annoyed Ben and me, but maybe he had found the perfect world for him. Inside, I really hoped he had because I knew I had. Who knew that Chase breaking up with me would be the best thing he could have ever done for me.

When the video ended, I decided not to masturbate. Instead, I put my vibrator back in my purse and got back to writing. I loved a good orgasm, but nothing turned me on more than writing the perfect combination of words. I wrote and wrote all night. I never slept and paid no attention to what time it was until my phone rang. I knew it was Ben from the ringtone so I answered it saying, "Hello."

Ben said on the other end of the line, "Good morning, my darling."

I asked, "What time is it?"

Ben said, "It's just after ten."

I asked, "Really?"

Ben said, "Did I wake you?"

I said, "No, I haven't slept yet."

Ben asked, "Why haven't you slept? Did you have a party in your empty apartment?"

I said, "A writing party. I wrote all night long, honey!"

Ben said, "That's great!"

Sincerely, I was able to say, "Ben, I love you. I really, really love you."

Ben laughed a little and said, "Hearing that is music to my ears. I love you too, darling."

I asked, "How did I get so lucky?"

Ben responded rhetorically, "How did I get so lucky?"

I said, "Come here. Come have sex with me

one last time in this apartment, please?"

Ben said, "I already picked up donuts and I am on my way. It's hard to stay away from you knowing you are just a few minutes away."

I said, "I'm already naked, but I'll go brush my teeth before you get here."

Ben joked and said, "But your morning breath is so sexy."

"Shut up, it's gross. I'm sure you've already showered and you smell fresh and so clean."

Ben said, "I've been up for hours so yes, I am fresh and clean. But, go brush your teeth. I'll be there in a few minutes."

I jumped out of bed and went into the bathroom to brush my teeth. I put my hand down on my pussy and then brought it up to my nose to smell and make sure there was no stench. It smelled a little funky so I jumped in the shower, splashing water everywhere because there was no shower curtain. I had soap in the travel bag I had, but when I got out of the shower I realized I didn't have a towel. I danced around a little trying to air dry and then used my clothes to dry off the remaining water. When I heard Ben opening the front door, I walked out of the bathroom and toward the front door. When he saw me standing naked he smiled, I smiled back and then ran to him. Once close enough, I jumped onto him and wrapped my legs around him. I said, "I missed you!"

Ben said, "Good! I didn't want to seem

pathetic because I missed you, too."

As Ben walked carrying me to the bedroom I said, "It's silly because just a couple months ago we spent so much time apart. I really hope we don't have to do that anymore."

Ben kissed me before he gently dropped me on the bed and said, "We won't. It's you and me, darling, every day, until death do us part."

"Fuck me, fuck me hard, you sexy man!"

Ben threw off his clothes quickly while I lay watching him. I was already naked and glad I was because there was nothing sexier than watching Ben get naked. He had such an exciting look on his face and in his quick movements when he knew he was about to get laid. Once Ben's clothes were off, he crawled on top of me with a smile. I said, "I'm all yours, what are you going to do with me?"

Ben said, "I think I'll start by spending quality time with your pussy."

I smiled as I said, "Excellent choice."

Ben kissed me for a few moments and then moved his way down my body, past my breasts and stomach before stopping on my pussy. I was glad I had showered because if I hadn't, I wouldn't be allowing him to use his tongue to pleasure me and warm me up. I looked down at Ben biting my lip while his tongue ran up and down my labia. He smiled at me with his mouth full of pussy and I smiled back. Watching Ben and feeling the slow movements of his tongue over my labia turned me on. I felt myself getting wet with cum and not just spit from Ben's mouth.

Ben kept at licking my pussy and sucking on my clit for several minutes. I enjoyed each moment and when he moved his face up by me, I knew that I had to return the favor. I kissed Ben before I pushed his chest and demanded him to stand up. I loved getting down on my knees and giving him a blow job while he was standing. I felt like I had more control of his cock and a man standing tall getting a blow job was always sexy.

I moved Ben's cock in and out of my mouth slowly, but took my mouth off it to discreetly spit on my hand. After my hand was full of spit, I rubbed Ben's balls with my wet hand and put his cock back into my mouth. I moved his cock in and out of my mouth while looking up at him and admiring how sexy he was. I took my other hand and placed it between my legs to gently rub my pussy. As I continued, I felt my pussy getting really wet, so wet I was sure my cum was dripping onto the ground. At least I hoped it was so I could leave a mark on a place I had called home for so long.

Once I knew Ben was inching up to the point of no return, I took my mouth off his cock for a small break. I wanted him to last so he could fuck me. We kissed for a few moments and while we were kissing Ben stepped in the drippings of cum that had come out of my pussy and hit the floor. He laughed and I laughed before we moved back on the bed. He led me to lay on my back, but I said, "This is farewell sex to my apartment so I want you to fuck me from behind."

Ben smiled as he said, "What Mrs. Wright wants, Mrs. Wright gets."

I turned over on my stomach and lifted up my hips before Ben penetrated my pussy from behind. I felt him grab my ass and squeeze it before he said, "Fuck, you are so fine, Audrey."

I smiled, hearing him swear and compliment me in the same sentence. There was no other combination of words that would've turned me on more in that moment. After a few minutes of slowly penetrating me while I lay on the bed on my stomach, Ben lifted my hips and I was soon on all fours. He kept moving his cock in and out of my pussy, but at a much faster pace. I was happy because I was ready to orgasm. I knew he could've orgasmed while his cock was in my mouth, but he held out to fuck me in a way I'd always remember as the last fuck in my old apartment. He moved quickly in and out of me and as he moved faster and deeper, my pussy got tighter and tighter. Once my pussy was hugging Ben's hard cock tight I moaned, "I'm going to cum."

Ben said, "Thank God, I don't know how much longer I can hold out."

I released my orgasm and as my pussy was pulsating, I felt Ben's cock begin to pulsate too, which created an even more intense orgasm in my body. After our orgasms subsided, we both crashed down on the bed to ride the waves of ecstasy and catch our breaths. I said to Ben, "Thank you."

Ben turned and smiled at me as he said, "No, thank you," before kissing me on my sweaty forehead.

I said, "We really make a great pair."

Ben said, "We are the perfect pair."

en and I had officially been living in our new, remodeled warehouse home for a couple weeks and I had approved the proof copy of my second memoir so I had no more excuses to not go see my gynecologist to get the lump on my breast checked out. I was overdue for my annual vagina tune up and the calls from Dr. White's office were becoming more annoying than Ben's persistence that I get the lump checked out so I made an appointment.

The morning of my appointment Ben woke me up with a kiss. He said, "Audrey, you need to wake up to go to the doctor today."

I asked, "Can I have five more minutes of sleep?"

Ben said, "No, time to get up. You definitely need to shower before you visit the gynecologist."

I pushed the covers off me and said, "Fine. I'll get up." When I looked at Ben he was all showered, dressed, and ready. I asked, "How long have you been up?"

Ben said, "A few hours. I wanted to get my work done so I could go to the doctor with you."

I said, "I told you that there's no way you are going to the vagina doctor with me."

Ben asked, "Why not? I want to be there in case you need me."

I said, "Not a chance, buster. I am doing this alone."

"Alright, but if there's anything wrong you promise you will call me right away?"

"Of course, I'm sure it's nothing so quit worrying."

I got up and got ready before heading out the door to see Dr. White. As I walked out the door, I realized that Dr. White was the only other man who would see my vagina for the rest of my life. I got in my new Bentley and as I pulled out of our garage, I realized I still wasn't used to driving such a fancy automobile. I enjoyed it though. The car had balls and I loved driving it like a bat out of hell.

When I arrived at Dr. White's office, I signed in and the receptionist asked me all sorts of questions. Good thing Ben briefed me on our new insurance before I left the house. I handed over my new 'married' insurance card and other paperwork that stated I was now Audrey Wright. After the receptionist handed me my documentation, I sat down in the waiting room. As I sat and waited, I looked at Facebook on my phone and secretly looked at all the pregnant women out of the corner of my eye. I hoped Ben didn't want to have babies anytime soon. We had never really talked about it because everything with us happened so fast. We touched on it a little when we were with his niece in California, but Carly was so cute she could make anyone want to have a child. I wanted kids in the future, but I wasn't ready to have one yet. Ben had his hands full just taking care of me so he didn't need a child to have to worry about too. As I sat in silence, I realized Ben and I should have "the baby talk" soon. It was probably something we should have talked about before we got married. I hoped he would be on the same page as me and give me a couple more years before we dove into that. I wanted a family, just not yet.

While I was in dreamland thinking about babies and how cute of a child Ben and I would create, the nurse opened the door and said, "Audrey."

I stood up and walked over to the nurse. She was new and not the normal nurse I had in the past. We walked down the hall and stopped at the scale. She asked me to stand on it so I did and when I did, she moved the little gadget to balance. Once it was balanced, it showed I weighed a hundred and one pounds. She said, "Oh dear, you need to gain some weight."

I said, "It's not so bad. I barely get my period anymore."

The nurse looked at my file and said, "You are on the pill so you should be regular."

I said, "Nope, and it's fantastic."

"Oh, honey, that is not healthy."

I said, "I eat all the time. I don't know why my weight is so low."

The nurse asked, "Are you working out more than usual?"

I laughed as I said, "I don't work out."

"At all?"

"No, not at all. I have sex a lot, but that's the extent of my attempt to work out."

The nurse's eyes widened before she said, "Oh my God, you are Audrey Buchanan, the writer! The one who wrote *Dating Chase Walker* and our very own Dr. White had a cameo in it."

I laughed as I said, "Yes, that's me."

"Girl, you are dirty."

I laughed again as I said, "We are all dirty, but I write about it."

"Ain't that the truth? That Chase was one hot cuckoo though. I can't wait for your second book. My friend just told me she heard it will be out late next month."

I said, "Yes, I actually just approved the proof copy the other day. You should be able to purchase it online even sooner."

The nurse said, "Next time you make an appointment to come here, tell the receptionist to let Shana know you are coming in. I want to bring my book with me so you can sign it."

I said, "You got it, Shana."

We got into the exam room and all Shana wanted to do was fish for answers about what was happening next in Audrey Buchanan's life.

I told her that my name was now Audrey Wright so a lot had happened. One moment she wanted the scoop, but the next minute she told me not to tell her because she didn't want me to spoil the next book. I was getting confused on if I should or should not tell her what was going on. I asked her if she wanted the scoop or not and she said she didn't and she wanted to wait to read about it in the next book. She handed me a gown and then on her way out the door she said, "Oh, I can't believe I just met a real life author!"

I undressed and then put on the gown before sitting down and waiting for Dr. White. As I sat, I took out my phone and saw a text from Ben that said, "Thinking of you, darling."

I sent back a text with a smiley emojicon and a couple minutes later Dr. White walked into the room. He said, "Audrey, the famous writer!"

I said, "Hi, Dr. White."

"How are book sales?"

"Slowing down a little, but the second book comes out soon so that should boost sales of the first one too."

"Did I get a cameo in book two, too?"

I said, "No, sorry not in the second book. This visit might make book three though."

Dr. White asked, "Oh, so the story continues?"

I said, "We'll see. I started something, but I'm not far into it."

Dr. White said, "I'll be on the lookout for them. My wife is a big fan. She was laughing so hard when she read the chapter about your visit. I'll be sure not to run out on you again this time."

I said, "Good. It's not very comfortable sitting with your crotch cranked open."

Dr. White asked, "What are we doing today? Are you just here for your annual exam?"

I said, "Yes, just my annual tune up and my husband would like you to check out this lump we found on my right breast. I think it just feels weird because of my implant, but it will get him off my case if you tell me all is okay."

Dr. White said, "Alright, let's check that first. Lie back." I lay down and opened my gown as Dr. White felt my breasts. He continued talking by asking, "You got married? I see it wasn't to Chase since your last name is now Wright."

I said, "Yes, Chase is out of the picture."

"Good, good, he had some issues it seemed. Tell me about your husband."

Dr. White kept feeling me up while I told him how wonderful Ben was. When he was finished, he assisted me in closing up my gown and asked, "How have you been feeling lately? It looks like you lost some weight."

I said, "I feel okay. I've been tired more than usual, but I have been traveling a lot and we just moved. Now that we are settled in I am sure I will get more rest."

"I'd like to get you scheduled for a mammogram. It will answer any of my concerns."

I asked, "What concerns?"

Dr. White said, "I'm just being cautious, Audrey. You do have a pretty large lump in your breast and what kind of doctor would I be if I didn't look into it fully?"

I asked, "It's probably nothing though, right?"

Dr. White said, "Let's not worry about it until the mammogram gives us more information."

Dr. White went to the end of the table and I put my legs in the stirrups for the dreaded vagina exam. I felt him crank open my crotch so I stared at the ceiling trying to think of things to distract me from the uncomfortable things happening down in my vagina. I decided to strike up more conversation when I asked, "Dr. White, can I ask you a non-vagina and non-boob related medical question?"

Dr. White said, "Sure thing, Audrey. What's on your mind?"

I said, "Well, the back story is that my ex-boyfriend, Chase, showed up at my wedding about two months ago. He was acting all loony and grabbed my upper arm to pull me to go with him. He left a black and blue mark on my arm and it swelled up. The black and blue mark went away, but the lump is still there. Is it something I should be concerned about?"

Dr. White stood up and took off his gloves. He walked over by me and asked me to put out my arm. I said, "Come on, man, did you really just leave my cooter cranked open again?"

Dr. White said, "Sorry, but let me feel this lump on your arm."

Dr. White felt around on my upper arm and then went back down by my vagina. As he was putting on a fresh pair of latex gloves he said, "I want you to go see a specialist as soon as possible, Audrey."

I asked, "About the lump in my arm that Chase gave me? I'm not being abused so I don't need a psychiatrist."

"No, Audrey, I think there's something more going on and I want to be sure. I am going to call my good friend Dr. Meredith Gasser to get you in as soon as possible. The lump in your breast raised concern to me, but the lump in your arm too makes me very concerned. I don't want to scare you, but I want to stress that this is something that needs to be looked at right away."

I got nervous and I could feel that nervousness growing in my stomach. I asked, "Do you think its cancer?"

Dr. White said, "I want to be able to rule that out as soon as possible."

I didn't want to talk about the "what if's" so I tried to lighten the mood and said, "Are you really sending me to person named Dr.

Gasser?"

Dr. White apparently didn't catch on to what I was saying and he said, "Yes, Dr. Meredith Gasser."

I said, "Dude, Dr. Gasser? Like the fart?"

Dr. White finally chuckled a little and said, "I've never thought about that before."

I said, "Come on, it has never ever crossed your mind that her name is Gasser? Man, my mind is really something else."

Dr. White said, "That, Audrey, that it is. Now I don't want you to go home worried. I will call Meredith myself this afternoon and then call you with a time to go into her office. I'll have the receptionist write down the address to her office before you leave."

I left the office and when I got in my car, I started crying. I tried to joke and ignore the fact that the word 'cancer' had just been spoken about in reference to my body, but I was fucking scared. One moment he was just going to send me off for a mammogram and the next he had me going to a specialist as soon as possible. I stopped for a donut on my way home to make myself feel better and when I pulled into our garage, I took a few deeps breaths to relax before I had to face Ben. When I walked inside Ben yelled out, "Audrey, I'm in my office."

I walked toward his office, taking another deep breath while I listened to him end his phone conversation. When I walked in through his office door he stood up and asked, "How did it go?"

My plan was to say that everything was fine; however Dr. White suggested I get a second opinion, but instead I burst into tears. In my cry, I mumbled out, "I have to go see Gasser."

Ben hugged me as he asked, "You have to gasser?"

I mumbled again saying, "No, I have to see Gasser."

Ben hugged me and let me cry for a few more minutes before he asked anymore questions. Once I started calming down, he led me to take a seat on the couch in his office. He handed me a tissue and then walked over to the cabinet and mixed me up a vodka 7Up. He was so good to me, always. He then poured himself a glass of whiskey straight up as he said, "It sounds like I might need this."

Ben came over and sat down next to me before he asked me to walk him through what had happened. I calmly did, but a few tears snuck out of my eyes as I explained. When I was finished, Ben said we had nothing to worry about until we met with Gasser. When he said, 'Gasser' I couldn't help but start to chuckle. Ben chuckled too as he said, "Only you would get a doctor named Gasser."

Dr. White called that afternoon and said I was to be at Dr. Meredith Gasser's office at 11am the next morning. I laughed a little when he said, 'Gasser' and he said, "Gasser is always going to make you laugh, isn't it?"

I said, "I'm sorry. I'm really immature."

Dr. White said, "Keep smiling and laughing. Everything is going to be okay, Audrey."

The next day Ben went with me to see what Gasser had to say about the lump in my breast. He held my hand the entire time. I actually think he was more nervous than I was. Something was wrong, but I hoped it was nothing serious. I did some research online the night before and found that women found non-malignant lumps all the time, especially at my age. I figured Dr. White just wanted to be extra cautious to save his own ass by sending me to see Gasser.

We walked into Gasser's office and I was handed a bunch of forms to fill out. Ben helped me and it was actually a fun opportunity for him to get to know me. We still had so much to learn about one another because we sort of skipped that process by jumping into marriage so fast. Gasser's nurse came out and Ben and I followed her down the hall holding hands. He kept squeezing my hand, which I felt was a gentle reminder that he was saying he loved me.

We sat down in the exam room and the nurse took my blood pressure, temperature, and asked me a bunch of questions. When she left the room I said to Ben, "Let's have sex real quick before Gasser gets in here."

Ben said, "Audrey, come on now. I love that you want to have sex all the time, but don't be using sex as a way to ignore what is going on."

I said, "I'm not trying to pretend like I am not about to be felt up by Gasser, I just think I look really hot in this medical gown so I figured you'd want to fuck me."

"I do want to fuck you most of the time, but right now I just want to make sure you are okay. I am so nervous right now I couldn't get my dick up if I tried."

I said, "Stop being nervous. Everything is going to be fine."

Ben said, "Being nervous is my job in this relationship."

I asked, "Your job?"

"Well, not my job. It's one of the things I handle. You handle the humor and keeping things sexy."

"You got screwed. I got the fun stuff."

Ben said, "That's why I love you. I'm good at finance and logistics. You, well, you are good at staying easygoing. You balance me out."

I said, "Good, but Ben, I have to tell you something."

"What's that, Audrey?"

I said, "Thank you for being nervous for me. I'm too scared to get nervous. I think denial is better for me right now."

Ben said, "Whatever Gasser says when she gets in here, we can handle it. We're a team."

I said, "Ben, I really love you. Like really,

really love you" before I leaned over and gave him a kiss. Ben said, "I don't think I'll ever be able to express to you how much I love you. You are the best thing that has ever happened to me."

I was smiling and giving Ben a look of endearment when Gasser walked into the exam room. One look at Gasser and I knew this woman meant business. Gasser's makeup-less face showed no emotion, but her hair looked like it had been rocking out since the late eighties. She wore black slacks under her white coat and a pair of Crocs. Just by looking at her I knew she wouldn't be fucking around and I was about to get whatever was coming at me straight up. Gasser said, "Afternoon, Audrey. White told me what's going on. I am going to do a quick exam and then we will take it from there."

I said, "Okay, Dr. Gasser. Do you need any more information?"

Gasser looked at Ben as she asked, "Who are you? The boyfriend?"

Ben said, "I am the husband, Ben."

Gasser said, "Alright, Audrey, lie back on the table. Husband, you can stand on the other side of the table and hold her hand if you'd like."

Ben walked to the other side of the table and took my hand. He squeezed it a few times before Gasser started moving her hands around my breast. When she started, I looked at her face for some sort of reaction to what she was feeling, but I quickly realized that Gasser had zero emotion in her face, body or words so I looked up at Ben. He smiled at me when I looked at him and I smiled back. As I looked at him, I still couldn't believe how lucky I had been to have the most amazing guy in the world fall in love with me. *Me!* Of all the women out there, he loved me.

As I was in la la land thinking about how I had the most amazing husband in the world, Gasser said, "Alright, Audrey, let's cut to the chase."

I said, "Gasser, you don't fuck around, do you?"

Gasser said, "No, Audrey, I'm brutally honest and I get things taken care of so my patients can put their minds at ease and get back to living."

Ben said, "I like it. You are speaking in my terms. So, what's the deal, Doctor?"

Gasser said, "You are not wearing any lotions, deodorants, perfumes, etc...? Correct?"

I said, "Nope, couldn't you smell my body odor when you lifted up my arm?"

Gasser said with seriousness, "I could not."

I said, "Oh, good."

Gasser said, "I see no jewelry. Thank you for listening to the instructions before coming in."

I said, "You are welcome."

Gasser said, "We are going to move forward

with the mammogram. Seeing that breast cancer runs in your family, I would like to test for the BRCA gene, but that test can be pricey and isn't always covered by insurance. We can hold off until after the mammogram if you want to wait."

Ben cut in, "Money is no object. Whatever you think is best to get answers as soon as possible."

Gasser said, "It is a simple blood test for Audrey, but the test results can guide us. Audrey, what would you like to do?"

I said, "If you guys think it's good to do then let's do it."

Gasser said, "I'll send the nurse in to draw your blood and then a technician will come get you to do the mammogram. I'll be in touch with you next week."

Ben asked, "Next week, like early in the week on Monday or late in the week on Friday?"

Gasser said, "You will hear from me by Friday." For the first time I saw some emotion grow on Gasser's face when she said, "Relax, everything will be fine. All these tests are just precautionary measures so I can make sure you live a long and healthy life."

Gasser showing a little emotion actually helped me to feel better. I liked that she functioned like a robot, but seeing a little emotion made me know she cared. The nurse came and drew my blood and then Ben and I waited for over a half hour for a technician to come get me to do a mammogram. I asked Ben if he wanted to have sex while we were waiting, but he looked at me like I was crazy. Instead, we talked about how I should tell my parents. Ben thought I should let them know what was going on, but I insisted we wait until Gasser called with the results of the mammogram and BRCA gene test. I was able to convince Ben that waiting was the best option.

Ben kissed me before I left the room for my mammogram and then we walked in different directions. He had to go out front to the waiting room until I was finished. When I got in the room where my mammogram was going to be performed, my eyes widened with intimidation as I looked at the machine. The technician told me not to worry and that the process was rather quick and painless. The technician was a fucking liar. She put my breast in the machine and it squished the fuck out of it. When the machine squished my breast, it was not only cold, but hurt.

When she finished squeezing the crap out of my breasts with the machine, she had me sit down for a few minutes while she looked at the images. She said they looked okay so I asked, "So there's nothing wrong? I'm good to go?"

The technician said, "No, the doctor will let you know. I am saying we got images of what we need to see."

I said, "Oh, okay. Damn."

I walked to the front of the office and stopped by the desk to see if they needed anything else. They didn't so I was free to go. When I walked out the door, Ben was sitting in a chair, but quickly stood up when he saw me. He asked, "How did it go?"

I said, "It fucking hurt."

Ben said, "Based on the research I just did on my phone, it sounds like mammograms are not very comfortable."

I said, "The technician lied and told me it was painless."

Ben put his arm around my shoulders and we walked out the door. While we were walking Ben said, "Why don't we leave for California tomorrow instead of Monday? We can spend a couple days on the beach before you have to meet with the production team to work on the screenplay."

I said, "That does sound nice."

Ben said, "Good, let's go home and pack."

On our drive home from Gasser's office, Nikki texted saying she wanted to go out that night. I hadn't been out with Nikki and Bree much so I told Ben I was going to meet them for dinner. I invited him to join us because I felt bad he hadn't had much time to make many new friends in Chicago, but he said a girl's night out would be good for me. He also thought it would be good for me to talk to Nikki and Bree about what was going on. I didn't want to tell anyone yet, but I knew Ben was probably right and their support could be helpful.

I wanted to lighten the mood so after we pulled into our garage and I got out of the car, I ran around to the other side and jumped up on Ben, wrapping my legs around him. I kissed his lips and said, "Fuck me right here, right now."

Ben kissed me back while holding me and walking a few steps toward the Bentley. He set me down on the hood of the car and then pulled my shirt off over my head before unhooking my bra. I sat bare breasted, watching as Ben took his shirt off. Once his shirt was off, I grabbed his belt buckle to pull him closer to me. I unbuckled his belt and pulled his pants down a little before letting them drop to his ankles. He leaned toward me and pulled my pants down. As I sat naked on the hood of the car, Ben looked at me and told me to scoot back. I told him I didn't want to put a dent in the hood of the car, but he said he didn't care. He just wanted to look at my sexy body, naked and sprawled out on the hood of the car. I obliged because his words made me feel sexy and turned me on and to be honest I could care less if I put a dent in the hood of my car. If I did, it would be a nice reminder of me having sex with Ben on it whenever I saw it.

As I sat in the middle of the hood of the car, I took my left hand and put my fingers in my mouth. I got them wet with spit before putting them down on my pussy and rubbing my clit. I slowly moved my fingers around and when I looked up at Ben I could see his cock growing harder. His cock usually got rock hard the moment we began making out, but I knew his mind was still elsewhere. I had to do something to get his mind off the possibility that I could have breast cancer. Ben put his hand on his cock as he watched me and began pleasuring himself. Watching him pleasure himself turned me on. I began moving my fingers around my pussy at a faster rate and I could feel my pussy getting wet so I stuck a finger inside to get my finger wet with cum. I moved my finger around and as I did I heard Ben moan. When I pulled my finger out and rubbed the cum on the lips of my pussy, Ben crawled on top of me and said, "I have to put my cock inside of you, now!"

Ben penetrated my pussy and I let out a moan in pleasure. He moved in and out of my pussy and it felt amazing, but I couldn't concentrate because the hood of a car was not the most comfortable thing to be lying on. With every thrust inside of me, my breasts would bounce and they were sore from the mammogram. I wanted Ben to get off so I was trying to hold out, but as I was sitting there I thought: *Fuck this. I want to get off too.* I gently pushed Ben off of me and then scooted off the hood of the car, leaving a small smear of cum behind me. When I stood up I turned around, bending over on the car. I said, "Fuck me like this."

Ben penetrated me from behind and

pushed his cock in and out of my pussy. Getting off of the hood of the car helped with my back issue, but my breasts were still bouncing. I held on to the car with my left hand and then gently held my breasts with my right arm to keep them from bouncing. I was finally ready to enjoy getting fucked when Ben said, "I'm going to cum."

I wanted to get off, but I knew there was no way I was going to be able to get myself to that point before Ben blew his load. I decided to just ride it out and said, "Cum for me. Cum hard!"

A second later I felt Ben's cock pulsate in my pussy. When he finished I stood up a little and put my arm behind me to wrap around his neck. He moved in close and kissed my neck. We stood there for a few moments and then Ben pulled his cock out of my pussy. It sort of plopped out because it had started to lose girth.

O ur weekend in California on the beach was relaxing, but come Monday I was busy all day and well into the night, working on the screenplay for the movie, *Dating Chase Walker*. I liked what the screenwriter had come up with, but I wasn't overly enthused by it. Scene by scene, we went over and over the dialogue and I pushed for what I wanted, but the producer had the final say and she was happy with the way it was. Come Wednesday night, after three sixteen-hour days, I realized it was going to be what it was so I decided to give up the battle. I was too tired to fight the little things anymore. When I got back to the hotel room that night, Ben wasn't there. I called him on his cell phone, but he didn't answer. I decided to walk downstairs to the bar to get a glass of wine and a bite to eat. I figured he had gone out to meet up with one of his friends in California and it made me happy knowing he was out and about. He hadn't had much time to make new friends in Chicago so he needed some "guy time."

I walked into the hotel bar and sat down on an empty stool at the bar. I ordered a glass of wine and while the bartender was pouring it, I heard Ben's voice. I turned around and saw that Ben was sitting with a very, I mean, *very* attractive woman. They were laughing and she was touching his leg. I turned around really quick to look at the bar again and hoped Ben hadn't seen me. I strained my ears and tried listening to their conversation. It was mostly just them laughing and, boy, did she have an annoying laugh. The laughing died down, but I kept listening to what they were saying when I heard, "Wait, I missed a call from my wife. I've been waiting to hear about her day. Let me step out for a moment and call her back."

I thought about turning around and walking over by them, but decided pretending like I didn't know they were there was a better idea. I sat at the bar and out of the corner of my eye I saw Ben step out into the lobby. A moment later my phone was ringing. I picked it up and said, "Hi dear."

Ben asked, "How was today? I want to hear all about it. Where are you? It sounds loud."

I said, "I just walked into the hotel bar to grab a glass of wine and a bite to eat to unwind."

Ben asked, "At our hotel? How could I miss seeing the most beautiful girl in the bar?"

I knew what his answer was, but I still asked, "Are you downstairs in the hotel bar, too?"

Ben didn't answer, but a moment later I felt

him come from behind me and kiss my cheek. I turned around and then he kissed me on the lips. He said, "Tell me all about today? Are you going back tomorrow?"

I said, "No, I'm all finished. They are going to do what they are going to do so I'm just going to let them." I continued by asking, "What are you doing down here?"

Ben said, "I ran into an old friend from high school. How crazy is that? Come with me. I want to introduce you."

I said, "Hold on, let me pay my tab."

Ben waved to the bartender indicating to add my drink to his tab and the bartender waved back. Ben said, "Come on. Don't worry about it, I have it covered."

I took Ben's hand and walked over to the absolutely gorgeous blonde girl he had been talking to. She stood up when we walked up to the table and I swear she had to be six feet tall. I was wearing a tank top from Target, old comfortable jeans, and flip flops while this girl was dressed to the nines in designer clothing. Ben said, "Kelly, this is my wife, Audrey."

What the fuck was with the name Kelly? The only other woman I had ever been jealous of was that girl Kelly that Chase went on a date with during the time we were together. Now, I was standing here jealous of another girl named Kelly who moments ago had her hand way too close to Ben's cock for my liking. Kelly said, "Oh, my God, the famous Audrey! Ben has been talking about you all night long."

Kelly saying Ben had been talking about me all night made me feel a little better, but it was still uncomfortable being face-to-face with a woman who I knew wanted to fuck my husband. Ben said, "Let's sit down."

All three of us sat down together. Ben and Kelly mostly talked about their high school years. I liked hearing about Ben's awkward past, but hated seeing the way Kelly looked at Ben. I noticed myself moving closer and closer to him with each word she spoke. When she laughed and grabbed his leg with her hand I wanted to smack it away, but I remained calm and just waved to the server to bring me another glass of wine. I sat there just listening to their reminiscing and I liked seeing Ben so happy laughing about old high school moments, but it was like he didn't have a clue about what she was doing until she grabbed his wrist while laughing. I saw him pull his arm away before he said, "I didn't realize how late it was. Audrey and I should get going. I was very nice to see you again, Kelly."

Kelly said, "No, don't leave. The night is so young and we have a lot of catching up to do still."

Ben said, "I want to go upstairs and catch up on my wife's day."

I thought to myself: *Boom, there was no better comeback*. Ben stood up and then put his hand out to assist me up. He gave Kelly a hug in which she held on for far too long before he led me away from the table. The server was walking back with my glass of wine so I grabbed it off the tray and continued following Ben. I wondered about our tab, but when Ben gave a wave to the bartender on our way out, I figured he had it under control. When we got in the elevator, Ben kissed me before he said, "I'm sorry if that in any way made you uncomfortable. I thought we were just catching up, but I realized she was acting inappropriately."

I said, "I was a little uncomfortable, but when you said you needed to catch up with your wife, well, that was awesome. You told her like a boss!"

Ben laughed before he said, "I am really sorry. I never meant to put you in an uncomfortable position."

I said, "It wasn't you. She is so pretty and flirty and that's what was intimidating."

Ben said, "She's nowhere near as beautiful as you."

I smiled at Ben and said, "I don't know how I got so lucky, but Ben you *ARE* the best thing that has ever happened to me."

Ben said, "I hope so, darling, because the feeling is mutual. Now, tell me about your day."

I said, "Nope, we are not talking about our days until after we have sex."

The elevator door opened and Ben said, "Last one to the room is on top!"

We ran down the hall like rowdy kids and when we got close to the door to our room I gave Ben a little push sideways to beat him, but he reached his arm out and touched the door at the same time as me. I said, "Looks like we are going fifty-fifty on being on top tonight," before we leaned in and began kissing. Lip-locked, we walked into the room over to the bed, pulling off articles of clothing with each step that we took. When we got to the bed, we finished undressing one another. Before we crawled onto the bed Ben said, "I am a gentleman so do you want to be on top first or would you like me to?"

I said, "You on top first and then I'll take over."

Ben guided my body onto the bed and then crawled on top of me. He kissed my lips for a moment and then moved his mouth down my neck. I thought it was sexy he was heading to spend a little time with my breasts, but after he licked my nipples a little he kept moving his tongue down my stomach. I said, "No, it has been a long day and I am sure the smell down there isn't pleasant."

Ben said, "I'm sure you taste amazing. Relax and let me enjoy your pussy."

I tried to forget about my pussy possibly being rank and enjoyed the movements of Ben's tongue on my labia. He moved slowly up and down before sucking on my clit. I loved the way he warmed me up and got my juices flowing. When I felt myself getting wet, Ben moved his lips back up my body to my neck. While he was kissing my neck, I felt him push his cock inside of my pussy. I moaned in pleasure, enjoying the initial penetration. Ben moved his cock in and out of my pussy while looking at me. I looked back at him with a look of endearment, but it was getting too serious for me so I pushed him over and onto his back. I sat up and moved my hips up and down on his cock. I closed my eyes as I put my hands up to play with my hair. Ben said, "Fuck, you are so beautiful. I love when you ride my cock."

I continued moving my hips up and down, enjoying how deep his cock went inside of me when I was on top. Not only did I love the way his cock rubbed my clit, but it hit a different spot deep inside of me. I continued moving faster with each thrust. I felt my pussy tightening up so I guided Ben's hands to hold my hips. Even if he wasn't controlling the movements of my hips, I liked feeling like he was. I loved a sense of sexual control over my body; it was such a turn on. As Ben squeezed my hips with his hands, my pussy squeezed his cock. I thrust my hips faster and faster, feeling both Ben's hands and my pussy become in sync until Ben said, "I'm going to cum."

I moaned, "Me too," right before I felt my pussy pulsate over Ben's cock. As my pussy was pulsating, I felt his cock pulsate and his mouth release a roar of a moan. When the pulsating stopped, I moved off Ben's cock to lie down on the bed. I jokingly said, "Mission accomplished."

Ben said, "Accomplished perfectly." We lay quietly for a few moments catching our breaths before Ben continued by saying, "Since you are finished working on the screenplay, can we go see my family tomorrow before we head back to Chicago?"

I said, "Of course. I thought the plan was to see them this weekend anyway."

"It was, but we can leave tomorrow to go see them now that you are finished."

"I'd love to go sooner."

The next morning Ben and I checked out of the hotel and took the scenic drive down the coast to Laguna to Ben's sister's house. Carly was still at school when we arrived so we settled in by having a glass of wine in the backyard with Catherine. Ben didn't drink because he wanted to pick Carly up from school, but Ben's sister and I each had a glass. After Ben left to get Carly, Catherine said to me, "I heard what's going on with the lump in your breast. Ben said you guys didn't want to tell anyone yet, but he told me. I think it is just because he is nervous and he cares about you. He also knows that a couple years back I had a scare with a lump in my breast. It turned out to be nothing, luckily, but I want you to know if you need someone to talk to, I am here."

I was a little surprised by Catherine being nice to me. I said, "Thank you. We are still waiting on test results so right now I'm not sure what to expect."

Catherine said, "I'm sure everything will be fine. No need to worry."

I actually hadn't been thinking about the lump in my breast at all the last few days until Catherine brought it up, but knowing she had the same scare and everything turned out fine made me feel a little better. Yet, I still felt anxious at the same time. I excused myself for a moment and walked over to the pool house where Ben and I were going to stay. I took my phone out of my purse and decided to call Gasser's office to see if she had an update for me. The wine had made me a little tipsy and emotional so I wanted to get any kind of answers out of her I could. When I called Gasser's office I was put on hold for several minutes before Gasser got on the line. She said, "Hi Audrey, I was going to give you a call later today, but I understand why you might be anxious for results."

I said, "Yeah, it has been on my mind today so I wanted to see if you had an update for me."

Gasser said, "I didn't like what I saw on the mammogram films and you tested positive for the BRCA gene so I'd like to do the fine needle aspiration on you next week."

I asked, "What's a fine needle aspiration?"

Gasser said, "It's a biopsy of the tumor in your breast. It is done with the help of an ultrasound where I use a fine needle to take out a biopsy for testing."

I asked, "How can you do that without popping my breast implant?"

Gasser said, "The ultrasound will guide me. I've done this test hundreds of times so there's no need to worry."

I said, "Okay" before I asked, "Dr. Gasser?"

Gasser said, "Yes, Audrey."

I asked, "Am I going to be okay?"

Gasser said, "You are going to be great. I'll be sure to do everything I can."

I said, "Thank you."

Gasser said, "I am going to transfer you back to the receptionist to schedule an appointment for next week."

Gasser transferred me and I set up an appointment for late Tuesday. When I hung up the phone I began crying. I hoped that when I talked to Gasser she would tell me all was well and I had nothing to worry about; however not only did she not like what she saw on the mammogram films, but I had tested positive for the BRCA gene. I curled up in a little ball on the bed and cried until I heard Carly's voice outside. I jumped up from the bed, wiped the tears from my eyes and used my shirt to wipe the boogers off my nose. Carly ran into the pool house and right up to me to give me a big hug. She said, "I missed you, Audrey!"

I quietly said, "I missed you too, Carly."

Carly asked, "Were you crying?"

I said, "No, I wasn't crying. I just got

something in my eye and it really hurt."

Carly said, "I got sand in my eye once and it really hurt."

I said, "Maybe it was sand."

Carly grabbed my hand and said, "Let's go play. I got a new soccer ball we can kick."

I said, "You go ahead. I am going to put some shorts on because I shouldn't play soccer in a dress."

Carly said, "Good idea. I'm not allowed to play in a dress either."

I said, "Okay, go get your soccer ball and I'll be right out."

Carly ran out the door and I heard her say, "Uncle Ben, Audrey got something in her eye, but she is going to play soccer with me after she puts shorts on. I'm going to go get my new soccer ball."

I heard Ben respond, "Okay, I'll go make sure Audrey's eye is okay and we will be right out."

Ben walked into the pool house and when he looked at me he looked a little scared. He asked, "Did you talk to Gasser?"

I started crying again and said, "I have the BRCA gene, Ben."

Ben said, "That's not so bad. It's good we know now."

I said, "Gasser didn't like what she saw on the mammogram films so I have to go get a needle put in my boob next week." As I continued I broke down and said, "I'm too young for this!"

Ben hugged me as he said, "You are young and that makes you resilient. We are going to get through this and be even stronger than we are now."

I said, "Ben, you picked a lemon of a wife."

Ben leaned back from our hug and looked seriously at me saying, "Never say that again. I got the most perfect and amazing wife. I love you and I am going to be by your side through every single step. Everything is going to be okay."

I asked, "What if I have to get chemotherapy and I lose all my hair? Will you still love me?"

Ben laughed when he said, "You have great hair, but I definitely did not marry you for your hair."

I said, "But if I have cancer, this could go on for years."

Ben said, "And every year you struggle I will be standing next to you. Wouldn't you do the same for me if the roles were reversed?"

Blinking I said, "Of course, I would."

Ben said, "Then quit questioning me. We are a team and we are going to listen to Gasser and do everything we can to make sure you are healthy."

We arrived back in Chicago on Monday night and on Tuesday morning we went to Gasser's office so she could stick a needle in my boob. On the phone, Gasser told me it was a fine needle biopsy so I assumed it would be like an acupuncture needle and it wouldn't be painful, but I was wrong. There was nothing fine about the needle she stuck inside my breast and moved around. I was lucky to have Ben by my side through the entire procedure. Somehow, looking him in the eyes distracted me from the pain and worry that one wrong move would pop my breast implant. The moment Gasser said she was done I breathed a sigh of relief. Ben asked, "Now what?"

Gasser said, "Now I am going to take the biopsy of the small lump near Audrey's armpit to make sure there is nothing going on with her lymph nodes."

I said, "Fuck, I forgot about that lump."

Gasser said, "It will only take a moment. Continue to lie still."

I continued to lie still as Gasser stuck a needle in my arm near my armpit, which hurt worse than the breast. I took some deep breaths to help me relax and when she said she was finished I asked, "Now what?"

Gasser said she would send the samples off to the lab and get back to me on Thursday. It was back to the waiting game, a game which I didn't enjoy playing. Wednesday I was busy meeting with my book agent and PR agent, Steven, so time flew by fast until Gasser called with the results. She had good news and bad news. The bad news was that the lump in my breast was a cancerous tumor, but it had not metastasized to my lymph node like she had worried so the lump in my armpit was not cancerous. Since it was a high grade tumor and I had tested positive for the BRCA gene, she wanted to do a double mastectomy as soon as possible. She asked if I planned to do breast reconstruction and of course I wanted new boobies to replace my old ones. I loved my fake boobs so I had to schedule a consultation with my plastic surgeon, Dr. Carroway. Once I had my consultation done, she would coordinate with him a time for them both to be in the operating room for my surgery.

When Ben and I hung up the phone after talking to Gasser, I felt overwhelmed. Lying in bed, Ben put my phone to the side and pulled me into his arms. We lay silently for a few moments before I heard Ben start crying. I began crying too. Still tight in Ben's embrace, we cried together saying no words, but letting tears release our worries, frustrations, fears, and love. Lying there in tears, we were connecting and that unspoken connection comforted me. I didn't like knowing that my health had worried Ben to tears, but feeling his concern through our connection made me know that with him by my side everything was going to be okay. I wasn't alone in this because the man holding me felt everything I was feeling. I had an urge to lighten the mood and crack a joke because that's what I did in uncomfortable situations. I said, "I think I'm going to get huge new boobs. Like double D's or something ridiculous."

Ben laughed a little before he said, "No, please don't."

I said, "I'm kidding, I won't. I'm going to tell my plastic surgeon, Dr. Carroway, I want them to look exactly like they do now."

Ben said, "Good because I like them the size they are now."

I asked, "Now what, Ben?"

Ben said, "We got our good cry out of the way so now it's time to be strong. Let's call Dr. Carroway to schedule your consultation and then let's figure out how we are going to tell your parents."

I called Dr. Carroway's office to schedule a consultation and the receptionist said he was booked solid for the next three weeks. I explained to her what the consultation was for and she said she could get me in Monday afternoon. After that, I called my mom to invite my parents over for dinner that Saturday night. Ben and I thought it would be best to tell them at home in case my parents got emotional from the news.

Saturday afternoon Ben was in the kitchen attempting to cook up a great meal for my parents when he said, "I should've hired a chef for the night."

I said, "Come on. It can't be that hard. I'll stop pretending to clean the house and help you. How can I help?"

Ben said, "It's not that cooking is hard, but I want everything to be perfect. I don't think my steak marinade is right. I guess I'm just nervous."

I looked at Ben and said, "Don't be nervous. Everything is going to be okay. Trust me, they will just be glad I am not feeding them pizza."

Ben said, "I'm just so nervous to see your parents' reactions."

I said, "They are two of the strongest and most supportive people I know. Stop being nervous and think of how once we tell them we will have their support too." *Wow, I was sounding like the strong one instead of Ben, which was rare.*

Ben kissed me and as we kissed I put my hand over his cock and rubbed it through his pants. Ben said, "Audrey, we can't have sex right now."

I asked, "Why not?"

Ben responded, "I know that you have been

using sex to distract yourself from what has been going on. It's okay to be nervous about what is happening because cancer is serious."

I said, "Ben that's what I do though. I am freaking out inside and sex relaxes me. Please can we have a quickie?"

Ben said, "You know I'd do anything for you, right?"

I said, "Then please put your penis inside of me!"

Ben smiled and then kissed me passionately before he pulled my panties off letting them drop to the ground. I stepped out of them and then pulled the white sundress I was wearing off over my head. Once I was naked, I unbuckled the belt on his jeans while he pulled his shirt off over his head. We stood naked, kissing and caressing each other's genitals for a few moments before I turned around and slightly leaned over the kitchen counter. Ben went to penetrate me from behind, but I wasn't wet enough and his cock wasn't hard enough to penetrate me so he moved his lips down to lick my pussy and get me going. The quick circular motions of his tongue and knowing that my parents were going to knock on the front door at any moment turned me on. Ben said, "I love how fast you get wet for me."

I smiled as Ben moved his body back up and penetrated my pussy from behind. When he penetrated me he went deep at first, which made me moan loud. I said, "Keep going deep in my pussy."

Ben obliged and moved his cock deep into my pussy with force. I knew that Ben hitting my deep spot would make me cum fast and I wanted to cum to send endorphins through my body and help me relax before I told my parents their only child had cancer. Ben used his hands to move my hips while he fucked me. I yelled out telling him to spank me. He spanked me hard and it sent a jolt of arousal through my body. I said, "Spank me again."

Ben spanked me over and over and with each spank and thrust deep inside of me, I felt my pussy getting tighter and tighter. I said, "I'm going to cum."

Ben said, "Cum for me. Cum hard!"

I released my orgasm and while I was orgasming, Ben released his orgasm and it heightened mine. My legs began twitching and if I hadn't laid my body over the kitchen counter to relax, I probably would've fallen to the ground. As I was catching my breath I said, "That, oh wow, that was amazing."

Ben laughed before he said, "Yeah, I feel much more relaxed about talking to your parents now."

Still catching my breath, I said, "Me too. Now kiss me, you magic lover."

Ben leaned forward and I turned around a little to kiss him. We kissed for a few moments until we heard a knock on the front door. Ben pulled away from our kiss and said, "Crap, we better put our clothes on. Your parents are here."

Ben and I scrambled to get dressed and I ran over to open the front door. As I was running to the door I stopped and turned around to blow Ben a kiss and say, "I love you."

Ben smiled at me and said, "I love you, too."

When I opened the front door, my parents opened their arms to welcome me in for hugs. As I hugged my mom she asked, "Why are you all sweaty and flushed? Are you sick?"

I lied and said, "I was running behind so I had to get ready really fast. How was the drive?"

My father hugged me as he said, "That damn interstate ninety is always backed up near the airport. We would've been here on time if it wasn't."

My mom said, "It's a good thing we were late because Audrey wasn't ready yet."

My mom was always full of such sly little burns. I said, "Yes, thanks for giving me those extra minutes, traffic. They were much needed. Now come inside, Ben is in the kitchen."

My mom said, "I still don't know how you got a man who is not only financially responsible and good looking, but he can cook, too. In my day we were told the way to a man's heart is through his stomach."

I said, "Well, in my day the way to a man's heart is through his penis, Mom."

Sounding shocked, my mom said, "Audrey!"

I said, "I'm kidding, Mom. What do you guys want to drink? Ben went and picked up some really good wine today."

My mom asked, "Does he do the grocery shopping, too?"

I said, "Typically, but mostly because he has a strange fascination with the self-checkout."

My mom said, "You don't know how lucky you are."

I said, "Mom, for the first time in my life, I do know how lucky I am. Don't worry because I am not going to screw this up."

Ben cut in and said, "Hi Mom, don't worry about Audrey. Even though she doesn't cook, she is the perfect wife for me."

My mom walked up to Ben and gave him a hug. My dad then shook Ben's hand before doing a quick reach over man hug. After their hugs I repeated my question to my parents and asked, "So do you guys want wine or something else?"

Everyone agreed on wine so I walked over to our fancy wine cooler to pick out a bottle. I brought it to the kitchen counter to open it, but Ben said he would open it. Once I poured us each a glass, my mom asked for a tour of the house. I walked with her down the hall while Ben asked my dad to help him carry some of the food up to the rooftop deck. I showed my mom around and when we got into my library, she was in shock. She said, "Ben really has made all of your dreams come true."

I said, "I know, but I can't believe with all the books I've been hoarding over the years, I still can't fill a library."

My mom said, "You are pretty close. Just a few open shelves. I think you should save those for your published books."

I said, "I'm sure I'll have them full in the next couple of years."

We finished our tour and then went upstairs to meet Ben and my dad on the rooftop deck. The guys were talking about the Chicago skyline so my mom and I took seats on our newly purchased patio furniture. After my mom tried to convince me to start a rooftop vegetable garden to eat organically, she started talking my ear off about family updates. I listened while I gracefully drank my wine trying to muster up my courage. I felt myself starting to get nervous knowing that I had to tell my parents I had cancer and I was about to get a double mastectomy. When Ben walked over by us I think he sensed my nervousness because he refilled my wine and sat down next to me. He put his arm around me before he whispered in my ear, "I got this, darling."

My mom said, "You guys are so cute. Was he whispering sweet nothings into your ear, Audrey?"

Ben said, "Of course I was, but we also have

some news for you guys."

My mom jumped up in excitement almost spilling her wine everywhere. She said, "I knew it! I knew when we came here you guys were going to tell me you were pregnant!" My mom started doing a happy dance as she sang, "I'm going to be a grandma!"

Ben looked at me and then said, "Well..."

My mother interrupted him and said, "You have made me the happiest woman in the world!"

I said, "No, mom," but my mother wasn't listening. I looked at my father and when he looked at me he gave me a look like he knew something was wrong. Like the news we had for them wasn't good. I said, "Mom" again, but she was still dancing around. Finally, I yelled out, "Mom, I have cancer!"

My mom dropped down in her chair with a look of shock on her face. I felt bad I had just screamed out that I had cancer like that. My father stood up and then sat next to my mother putting his arm around her. He asked, "Cancer?"

I said, "Yes, breast cancer."

Ben said, "We've got it all under control though. The tumor in her breast hasn't metastasized and that's good news."

My mother said, "No, no, my baby can't have cancer."

I said, "Mom, it's going to be okay. We caught this all early so I am going to be just fine. I'm getting a double mastectomy and some new boobies in the next couple of weeks since I tested positive for the BRCA gene. After that, we will sit down with Gasser to find out what's next."

My dad asked, "Gasser?"

I laughed as I said, "Yeah, my doctor's name is Gasser."

My dad started laughing too. He said, "Only you would get a doctor named Gasser."

My mom whimpered, "This is no time to be laughing!"

My father and I had a tendency to use humor to help us cope and my mother hated it. Ben cut in and said, "I promise I am making sure Audrey gets the best treatment money can buy and support through this. She is going to come out of this stronger than ever."

My mom stood up and walked over to me. She put her hand out to have me stand up and then wrapped her arms around me while she cried. She cried hard. Hearing my mother cry brought tears to my eyes. In her tears, my mom mumbled, "You are the most important thing in the world to me. I don't want to see you hurting."

Ben stood up and hugged me from behind and my dad stood up and hugged my mom from behind. We stood there and cried in a big group hug for a couple minutes and with all the sadness in our hugging circle, I felt more love and it helped me. Ben was right when he said the sooner we told my parents the better because with each person that supported me I could only become stronger.

When the boogers in my nose became too much, I broke up our circle of tears and said, "Now that we got the tears out of the way, let's be strong. Please be strong for me, Mom and Dad!"

My mom said, "I need another glass of wine."

I said, "That's the spirit!"

My parents, Ben and I got drunk. I mean wasted; so inebriated that my parents had to stay the night in the guest room. It was one of the most fun nights I have ever had with my parents and even though I woke up with a terrible hangover, I didn't regret it one bit.

That Monday I met with my plastic surgeon, Dr. Carroway to discuss my mastectomy and breast reconstruction surgery. We talked to Gasser and scheduled my surgery for the following Tuesday so I had a list of things that I had been putting off with my book agent and PR agent to finally take care of. We met every day and made plans for promotions of the second book in my memoir series, *Time for Audrey Buchanan*, to start well after my recovery.

On Friday, Ben left for New York for two days to take care of some business. He wanted to get a few things done so he could be by my side during recovery from surgery. I spent Friday night home alone with wine while continuing to write my story. As I was writing, I came up with the title of this part of my story; *Loving Mr. Wright*. Ben had only been gone a few hours, but in those few hours I missed him so. I realized with each word that I wrote just how much I loved him. I had so much more story left to tell of my life ahead, but my story was no longer just my story. It was our story and I couldn't wait to keep on living and writing our story.

Saturday night I went out for a good old fashioned girl's night out with Nikki and Bree. We started with dinner at Fulton Market Kitchen and then went to the roof space at The Godfrey Hotel. As we sat at our table at The Godfrey, we cried like a bunch of drunk white girls. Not because we were drunk, which we were, but because Bree started talking about my cancer. We probably looked like fools to the people around us; however we didn't care because we were bonding in our own private little world. After we finished two bottles of champagne at The Godfrey, we headed over to the Underground where we popped another bottle of champagne.

I was enjoying myself thoroughly, but on my way to the bathroom I spotted Chase's girlfriend, Vivian, and I didn't want to deal with any nonsense. I was drunk and ready to go home anyway. When I got back to our table I told Nikki and Bree I was going to head home. Nikki tried to convince me to stay, but Bree said she was ready to go home too.

When Nikki's "new man" showed up, Bree and I left. The cab dropped her off first and then took me home. I was so tired and drunk that I don't remember walking into my house. The next thing I recalled was when I felt Ben crawl into bed with me. I rolled over mumbling, "You came home early."

He said, "It's me, Audrey."

When I heard the voice, I sat up quickly, completely freaked out. It was Chase. I said, "How the fuck did you get in my house? Get out!"

Chase said, "I know you have cancer."

I yelled, "Get the fuck out of my bed and my house, before I call the fucking cops."

Chase said, "You knew I would come. We have a spiritual connection that you will never have with another."

I said, "How the fuck did you get in my house?"

Chase began crying like he always did. I rolled my eyes as he said, "I knew all along something was wrong and I am sorry my senses weren't spot on."

I asked again, "How the fuck did you get in my house?"

Chase said, "I can heal you. Let me. Be with me."

I yelled, "Fuck, no! Chase, you had me and you left me because you wanted to chase the muff around. And to be honest, you leaving me was the best thing you could have ever done for me. If you hadn't, I may have never reconnected with Ben, the love of my life."

As Chase continued crying he said, "I am the love of your life, Audrey. You belong with me."

I said, "Chase, I am asking you nicely one more time to leave or I am going to call the police."

Chase put his head on the pillow and cried while he pounded his fists on the bed and said, "No, no, no! This is not how it is supposed to be. You were supposed to see my greatness after we broke up and come back to me wanting to share our love with anyone who wants to be with us."

I said, "Seriously, Chase, get the fuck out of my house."

Chase said, "You need to listen to me. I can heal you. God has blessed me with healing powers."

I said, "You are really starting to scare me. Get out or I am going to call the police."

Chase said, "I want to make love to you so you can feel my powers and energy. Once you feel it, you will be able to understand."

I asked, "Did you seriously just say that, Chase?"

Chase said, "Let me make love to you. I know I am the best lover you will ever have."

I said, "Chase, I don't get you. Now get out of my fucking house!"

Chase said, "You need to listen to me. People need to listen to me."

I said, "Nobody needs to do anything for you. What you need to do are things for your true self and to quit being a chameleon to try to get attention and fake love from other people. You are better than that. Do you know when I loved you most? It wasn't when you were buying me stuff with money you don't have. It wasn't when you were giving me amazing orgasms. It wasn't when I watched you on stage telling people bullshit. It was when you were sick. I didn't want to see you sick, but when you were sick I saw the real you."

Chase said, "Oh, so you want me to live my life sick and helpless?"

I said, "No, I think you should live your life as the real you. Quit going out and living a lie. Quit thinking you are a God or an Indigo Child or whatever. Go out there and live as the real you. I assure you that when you do, you will find the person who loves you, the real you, and *that* will be enough."

Chase said, "You did love me the way I am and that's why you belong to me."

I said, "Quit that 'belong to' fucking nonsense. I did love you, Chase. I loved you dearly, but nobody is going to be able to love you truly until you learn to love the real you. Stop making yourself into a character to try to succeed in life. Just be the real you and I promise that by doing that you will be happy and loved by someone so greatly that it will change your life."

Chase yelled out in tears, "Why don't you love me?"

I said, "I did love you and with time someone else will." I picked up my phone off the night stand before continuing; "Now I am giving you sixty seconds to get out of my house before I call the police."

Chase moved slowly, but got off my bed and began walking toward the door. When he got to the door he turned around and said, "I'll be sending you healing powers. Please open yourself to accept them."

Once Chase was out of my room, I walked out into the hall to listen to him exit out the front door. After he closed the door behind him, I ran down the stairs and locked the door before turning on the alarm system. I went back upstairs and called Ben to tell him what had happened. Ben was not pleased and he, too, didn't understand how Chase got inside our home considering we had the most expensive alarm system on the market. Ben said we needed to take legal action against Chase to keep him away and not just some signed document drawn up by a lawyer. Ben thought it was time to get the police involved. I agreed that things had gone too far and called the police while Ben was on the line with me. They sent two officers over and with Ben on speakerphone the whole time, I explained what had happened. The officers reviewed the security video footage and it showed Chase walk in the front door without any problem. This meant that not only did I forget to set the security alarm, but I forgot to lock the door in my drunken state.

The officers left the house and headed to arrest Chase for trespassing. After they left Ben used firm words with me for my carelessness. I didn't blame him for being upset and assured him it would not happen again. Even though Ben was upset with me, he ended our conversation with a gentle voice and a reminder of how much he loved me. After we hung up the phone I lay in bed for quite awhile thinking about how I screwed up while telling myself over and over that I needed to be more responsible.

I slept until almost one in the afternoon and then lay in bed writing for a good hour or so before finally getting up and showering. After my shower, I came up with the genius idea to surprise Ben with dinner. Ben had already warned me that I could not drink the night before my surgery so it would be the last night I could get my wine on.

I went to the store and bought meat, potatoes, spinach, and other little items. The only thing I knew how to make was my mother's famous meatloaf and spinach potatoes. I figured I'd be progressing by at least attempting to be domesticated and make a meal. I got home and poured myself a glass of wine before getting to cooking. Ben would be home a little after 5 p.m., which was way early to eat, but I had to deal with eating like I was eighty years old if I wanted to surprise Ben.

Ben texted me that he landed and was on his way home, which gave me just over a half hour to finish implementing my plan. Usually, I wasn't a fan of rainy days, but I was happy it was cold and rainy because it would make my night much sexier. I lit candles all over the living room and kitchen. After I was finished with that, I went into the garage to dig out the box of interestingly odd handmade gifts I got from my aunts for my wedding shower. I knew there was a ridiculously weird, but could be made sexy, apron in the box somewhere. I mean, any apron worn without clothes underneath it was a sexy apron in my opinion.

I went upstairs and took off my clothes before putting on the apron, which kind of smelled like my Aunt Flo, who smelled like a mix of cats and mildew. The smell would take my sexiness down a few notches so I threw it in the dryer for a couple minutes with an entire box of dryer sheets. As the dryer was going round and round I danced in only my heels in front of it in excitement for Ben to come home. When I heard Ben open the door, I took the apron out of the dryer and put it on before walking down the stairs. As I walked, I looked down at Ben with a smile. He said, "It smells good in here and... and are you wearing an apron? Only an apron?"

I said, "Yes, I am playing the role of a domesticated wife tonight. Do you like?"

Ben said, "I love some role play. Hold on, let me put my 'briefcase' down so I can give you a passionate kiss."

Ben put his pretend briefcase, which was actually his suitcase, down and then I ran into his arms and gave him a big kiss. After our kiss I said, "Your dinner is in the oven. Would you like a glass of wine or a cocktail while you wait?"

Ben asked, "How much time do we have?"

I stood on my tippy toes to look over the counter at the oven and said, "We have plenty of time."

Ben laughed as he said, "Good, I'll take a scotch on the rocks and a blow job."

I said, "Coming right up."

Ben said, "Wait, I was kidding."

As I walked toward the liquor cabinet I said, "I hope you weren't. Now take your pants off and sit down on the couch. Keep your dress shirt on. It's sexy."

Ben obliged while I poured him a hefty glass of scotch. After the glass was full of scotch and ice, I walked over to Ben trying to look sexy. When I got close, I handed him the glass and then gave him a long passionate kiss. He looked sexy, sitting there with nothing but a dress shirt on. I moved my lips from kissing his lips and then down his chest. My lips kissed his chest as I unbuttoned each of the buttons on his shirt until it was completely open before I moved my lips onto kissing his cock. I began with light kisses and licks, proud that his cock was growing with such little effort on my part.

I decided to stop teasing Ben and I put his cock in my mouth, deep. When his cock was deep inside my mouth, I moved my tongue around while I listened to Ben moan in pleasure. I knew what I was doing was good so I kept at it for a few moments before sliding his cock in and out of my mouth, slowly. I increased the speed of my movements as I felt the girth of his cock increase. I took my right hand and grasped his cock to move up and down with my mouth while I moved my left hand down on my pussy. I rubbed in a circular motion on my clit as I continued moving my mouth on Ben's cock. The movement of up and down with one hand and moving circular with the other reminded me of when I was younger and my friends and I would pat our heads and rub our stomachs. I had the pattern down, though, and I was enjoying myself.

Although I was turned on and I wanted to get laid, I wanted to get Ben off. I wanted to taste his cum in my mouth. I took my left hand off my pussy and used it to lightly massage his balls while continuing to move his cock in and out of my mouth. He said in a rather demanding voice, "Faster," so I moved my mouth in and out faster. Moments later he said, "Fuck, I am going to cum!" I thought to myself: *That was really fucking fast*, but I didn't say anything.

I looked up at Ben's face when he came and it was sexy. I was totally turned on, but I wanted to serve Ben so I didn't get selfish by leading him into getting me off. We had all night and I knew we'd be getting it on again. I swallowed Ben's cum and then took the glass of scotch off the table and took a sip to wash the cum down. As I was sipping on the scotch, Ben said, "Thank you."

I said, "Anytime you want a blow job, just ask. I like getting you off."

Ben said, "I am honestly the luckiest guy in the world. Come up here and kiss me!"

I stood up and gave Ben a kiss. While we were kissing, the timer went off on the stove so I pulled away as I said, "Dinner is ready! Stay here and enjoy your drink. Don't put your clothes back on. I'll call you in when the meal is on the table."

I went into the kitchen and took the meatloaf out of the oven. The potatoes and spinach got a little burnt so I only scooped the top part out and put that in the bowl. I got everything out on the table and then yelled out, "Darling, dinner is served."

Ben walked into the dining room with a smile. He said, "This is amazing, Audrey."

I said, "I'm glad you like it. I hope we don't get poisoned from my cooking, though."

Ben laughed, but assured me we'd be fine. We had a great night together, eating meatloaf and drinking scotch and wine. We probably drank too much, but we were celebrating us before I'd be stuck in the hospital and in bed for a couple weeks. After having sex on the dining room table, in the library, and building a fort in the living room, we decided to take a bath together. Ben assisted me in the tub and then we washed the sex and sweat off each other's bodies. As Ben was washing my back with a sponge his voice cracked as he admitted to me how nervous he was for my surgery. I turned around and kissed him before I said, "Nothing bad is going to happen. The surgery is going to be just like when I got my breast implants, only I'll need a little more recovery time for this."

Ben said, "I just wish it was me and not you."

I said, "I appreciate that, but everything is going to be okay. I'm going to come out of this with a brand new pair of boobs and I am going to look hot!"

Ben laughed before he said, "But I like the boobs you have now."

I said, "You are going to like my new boobs even more, I promise. You know what you should do before I get my new boobs though?"

Ben smiled at me before he grabbed my body and moved it toward him. Once I was close he motorboated my breasts and the bubbles blew everywhere. He said, "I don't think I've ever motorboated your breasts before! I'm glad I got to do that."

I said, "I don't think I've been motorboated since college, but that was fun. I was going to say that you need to titty fuck me."

Ben said, "You are always one up on me when it comes to sex and that's one of the many reasons why I love you," before he kissed me.

I said, "Well, you taught me to truly love so I owe you."

Ben said, "You owe me nothing."

I said, "Alright, fine, you owe me a titty fuck then."

Ben stood up and put his hand out to assist me out of the bathtub. He said, "If a titty fuck is what my wife wants, then a titty fuck is what my wife will get."

Ben led me out of the bathtub and onto the bed. I was still wet and had bubbles all over my body, which made it easy for him to slide his cock between my tits as I pushed them together. He moved his cock in the middle of my breasts and I squished them hard, but as I held them I could feel the lump and my mind started thinking about the cancer in my breast. I kept telling myself not to think about it, but it was hard to ignore. I stayed strong and let Ben enjoy the wetness between my breasts while I watched his cock get harder with each motion. Ben said, "Fuck, you are the hottest thing I have ever seen."

I wanted to respond saying something sexy, but my mind was still on the cancer in my breast pushing up on his cock. Ben kept at it for a few moments and then suddenly stopped. He said, "Something is on your mind."

I said, "Your cock is on my mind."

Ben said, "No, something else. Is the lump distracting you?"

I said, "Yes, I'm sorry. It's just hard to ignore when I can feel it with my hand and it is pushing up on your cock."

Ben moved off my body before he said, "Let's do this right."

I said, "What do you mean, right?"

Ben said, "With me looking at you and you looking at me."

I said, "Okay, you lead this time."

Ben did as I said and kissed my lips, slowly, before kissing my neck. After kissing my neck he stopped for a moment and looked at me. His hand was holding the back of my head, but he didn't say a word. He just looked at me and I looked back. I looked at him, admiring his eyes, admiring the strength I could see in his arms, admiring having his body near mine, and enjoying the connection I could feel between us. As we looked at one another, connected, Ben penetrated my pussy. He moved in and out of me slowly while keeping eye contact. We kept eye contact and part of me kept thinking how what was happening was weird, but another part of me was feeling something I had never felt before.

Ben continued penetrating me at a slow pace and without a thought my pussy was getting tighter and tighter. It was like I was reading a romance novel where the guy was reeling the woman into an orgasm with his thoughts and it was working. After slow penetration and eye contact for several minutes I whispered in Ben's ear, "I'm going to orgasm."

Ben whispered back, "Me too."

I released my orgasm and it was a slow release. It wasn't some powerful, body twitching moment. Instead, it was a long slow release that was prolonged when Ben came inside of me. When I finished I felt strange, not a bad strange, more of a feeling of serenity. Ben moved off me and lay down cuddling up to me. We weren't out of breath from heart pounding sex, but we lay relaxed from heartwarming sex. As Ben cuddled behind me, he kissed the back of my neck before saying, "I love you."

I said, "I love you, too."

Moments later I heard Ben snoring. I don't know how he could fall asleep after sex like that. I had never experienced sex that created satisfaction based on emotion. I always thought I had. I mean, I was in love with Ben and we had sex at least a thousand times before, times in which I felt more connected, but I had never felt like I did in those moments. I listened to Ben snore for a few minutes, but knew I wouldn't be able to fall asleep. I had just experienced, for the first time, true emotional sex. I made love, something that I had thought I had made before, but the love I thought I made ranked nowhere near what had just happened. I was feeling confused, scared, and delighted all at the same time.

I decided to slowly move out of Ben's cuddle and go downstairs. I poured myself a glass of wine and then went into my library to write. I sat down on the couch and looked up at the bookshelves still in awe that I had my very own library to sit and write in. I put a blanket on my lap and whipped out my laptop opening to part three of my story that I had titled *Loving Mr. Wright*. I read through the last few paragraphs that I had written, which were of my wedding day, and then I continued writing from there. I wrote about London, our new home, and my cancer diagnosis until I reached this point. The point in which I don't have anything else to reflect on, but I now can only think about the future. My future, a future that holds all the possibility in the world.

This chapter of my life doesn't end with me being left by a man who wanted my love at his convenience. This chapter doesn't end with me drowning myself in wine because the love of my life didn't show up at the top of the Empire State Building for my romance movie plan. This chapter of my story ends in love. It ends in belief that no matter what happens, I have someone by my side to love and support me through it all. What will come after my surgery I know will not be easy, but after the physical pain and hardship of it all subsides, there is a beautiful life to be lived with my "Mr. Wright."

So here I sit in a library full of books, a

room in which I only dreamed I would have, reflecting on all the right, write, and Wright in my life. I mean, I have cancer in my body, but I have never felt happier in my fucking life. I found what most spend their lives trying to find. I found the one, my soul mate, the man that makes me a better me. My grandmother was right and there is so much more of my story to tell and I can't wait to tell it.

Afterword by Ben:

A month ago today Audrey went into surgery and as they rolled her down the hall, she looked beautiful in her hospital gown and cap. I know, it sounds silly to say, but if you could see what I was seeing you would say she looked beautiful, too. The two hours that she was in surgery were the longest two hours of my life. Worry ran through me and to stay consistent with Audrey's honesty, I went to the restroom three times with massive diarrhea from nervousness. Luckily, the restroom was right next to the waiting room so I did not poop my pants.

When the doctor came out to tell me that the surgery went perfectly and that I could see Audrey, I felt such relief. I gave Audrey's parents each a hug and then followed the doctor into the recovery room. Audrey was loopy and kept telling me she couldn't wait to see her new boobs. When Audrey was released from the recovery room and rolled up to her hospital room, I was standing next to her, holding her hand the entire way. She fell asleep as soon as we got into the room so I sat next to her watching her sleep for hours. I didn't turn on the television, I didn't read any of the magazines, I didn't work; I just sat there, watching her sleep.

Audrey's parents came into the room and sat with me for a couple hours. We conversed, but it was hard for me to take my eyes off Audrey. They left just before midnight to go back to our house to get some rest, but I couldn't leave my Audrey. A little past two in the morning Audrey was finally speaking coherent words, they were words in which I could understand and help soothe her. All she wanted was for me to lie in the bed next to her. I gently helped Audrey move over and then cuddled up next to her. To be honest, I was grateful for her invitation into bed because I knew by holding her and feeling her next to me I could finally sleep.

Audrey and I slept in that bed until she woke up in the morning in pain. The moment I felt her moving, I was wide awake. She needed pain pills so I found a nurse to help relieve her pain as soon as possible. After she took the pain pills, I sat down in the chair next to her bed, but she insisted I crawl back into bed with her, so I did. I held her just the way she wanted me to hold her for the next few hours. She fell asleep, but I didn't. I couldn't because I was full of worry that she was in pain. When Audrey's parents came back to the hospital I got out of bed and went downstairs for coffee with her father while her mother sat with her. Nikki and Bree came by the cafeteria to say hello before they went to visit Audrey. Since there were quite a few visitors with Audrey, her father and I sat and talked in the cafeteria.

When Audrey's father and I got up to her room, the flowers I had ordered for her finally arrived. Since Audrey loved white daisies, I ordered two dozen vases full of them. After seeing them I realized it was a bit much, but if the room fit a million vases of white daisies I would have had that many delivered.

Audrey was in and out of sleep because of her painkillers so we sat and conversed until night came and one-by-one, visitors left. I liked having people there with me, but my only concern was Audrey and I wanted all my attention to be on her. When the room cleared, it was just Audrey and me and she was making some sense when she talked. We talked for a little while with me cuddled up next to her in bed until she said she was sleepy. I slowly ran my fingers through her hair until she fell asleep. Once I knew she was asleep, I closed my eyes and dozed off.

In the middle of the night I felt Audrey moving as if she was agitated. I asked what was wrong and she said her heart hurt. I noticed she was not breathing right so I yelled out for a nurse and pressed the button next to the bed requesting help. Moments later Audrey looked almost as if she was convulsing and that's when the nurse came in. The nurse yelled out some code and two other nurses ran in. They kicked me out of the bed and rolled Audrey away. I tried following them, but one of the nurses stopped me. Tears filled my eyes. I had no idea what was happening.

I stood in that room, alone, not knowing if I should call Audrey's parents for over an hour until a doctor finally walked in the room to tell me what was happening. He didn't need to say any words. Just the look on his face said it all. It was a look that the one I loved was gone. I fell to the ground in anguish even before the doctor spoke a word.

Audrey coded from a pulmonary embolism, a blood clot in her lung. The doctors revived her once, but she coded again on the table and that's when they lost her. I've never written anything except school papers and business documents in my life. After Audrey passed away and the funeral was over I couldn't bear spending another minute in our home so I went back to New York and then spent time in California to avoid seeing Audrey everywhere I looked. My body was physically hurting from missing her. I couldn't and I still cannot think of the right words to say to explain my love for Audrey and that's how I know it was true. Whenever I was around Audrey, whenever we spoke, whenever we were having sex, even whenever a thought of her ran across my mind it would consume me entirely with bliss. The day I received Audrey's letter to meet her at the Empire State Building, I literally danced around my condo like Tom Cruise in *Risky Business*.

Running away from the life I had with Audrey wasn't what I needed. I couldn't stop thinking about her and I needed to find a way to truly say goodbye to her. I decided to go back to Chicago to think, alone in our home. I walked into our home and smelled her clothes, I lay for hours crying in her library, I drank her favorite wine, and I let the vision of her walking to the front door in that white sundress before turning around to blow me a kiss run over and over in my head.

While I was immersed in my sadness listening to the song *Moon River* over and over while begging for God to give Audrey back to me, I opened her computer and the story, this story *Loving Mr. Wright,* came up. I knew she had been writing, but I never knew that this part of her story had been a documentation of our love and life together. With wine in my hand, I read every single word feeling so many emotions and when I read the last sentence that she wrote I broke down harder than I did at the hospital when I learned of her passing. I broke down harder than I did at her funeral. I broke down with so much sadness, my heart literally hurt and I felt like I could punch a hole through a brick wall. I didn't punch anything, instead, I wondered to myself what would Audrey do? I knew that in times of pain, Audrey wrote so I am writing this afterword to heal my heart the way she always healed hers.

This story is the greatest gift I have ever been given in my life. I showed Audrey affection with lavish gifts, but Audrey showed her affection for me in a much deeper way. Although thoughtful, my gifts were all tangible. Audrey, however, gave me the gift of making our love immortal through the written word.

I will end this as Audrey would by saying: So here I sit writing, which is something I have never done before. My eyes are full of tears, but I feel happiness inside knowing that the last of what Audrey wrote was pure joy. All I've ever wanted was to take on any sadness and hardship of hers and this story, well, she ended her story full of bliss for what was to come and that's what should live on.

"Living is like tearing through a museum. Not until later do you really start absorbing what you saw, thinking about it, looking it up in a book, and remembering – because you can't take it in all at once."

-Audrey Hepburn

www.ingramcontent.com/pod-product-compliance
Lightning Source LLC
Chambersburg PA
CBHW060229050426
42448CB00009B/1359

HIT ME ONCE
HIT ME TWICE

By
Brian S. Bentley

This is a work of nonfiction; the names of persons involved have been changed including the names of law enforcement officers interviewed.

COOL JACK PUBLISHING

LAPDAuthor@aol.com

Second Printing

For the purpose of this book, domestic violence is defined as repeated injury caused by a spouse, former spouse, or someone who is or has been sexually involved with the victim. Continuous verbal abuse is also included in the definition. The abuser can be male or female. This book will address the issue of males abusing females.

It is not the author's intentions to provoke fear or deter women from addressing abusive relationships. The purpose of this book is to heighten the awareness of people who are directly or indirectly involved in domestic violence situations. It is important we understand the victims and law enforcement that has the ultimate responsibility of protecting them.

Over half of the women murdered in the United States are killed by their husbands, ex-husbands, boyfriends or ex-boyfriends. You may not be aware, but someone close to you is, or may become a victim of domestic violence. Domestic violence incidents among women usually go undetected by friends and neighbors for years until the victim gets seriously injured. Many women find it hard to realize they are being abused. Abuse can come in the form of emotional cruelty, physical attacks or sexual abuse. The abuse usually begins with verbal attacks and then escalates to physical violence.